THE ACTIVATION DILEMMA

Reconciling the fairness and effectiveness of minimum income schemes in Europe

Amilcar Moreira

This edition published in Great Britain in 2008 by

The Policy Press
University of Bristol
Fourth Floor
Beacon House
Queen's Road
Bristol BS8 1QU
UK

Tel +44 (0)117 331 4054
Fax +44 (0)117 331 4093
e-mail tpp-info@bristol.ac.uk
www.policypress.org.uk

British Library Cataloguing in Publication Data
A catalogue record for this book is available from the British Library.

Library of Congress Cataloging-in-Publication Data
A catalog record for this book has been requested.

ISBN 978 1 84742 046 6 hardcover

Cover design by Robin Hawes
Front cover: image kindly supplied by www.stockxpert.com
Printed and bound in Great Britain by MPG Books, Bodmin

Para os meus pais. Longed a vista, mas perto do coração!

(To my parents. Out of sight, but close to my heart!)

Contents

List of tables and figures

Tables

Figures

List of abbreviations

ABW	*Algemene bijstandswet* (the Netherlands)
ALMP	Active labour market policy
BSHG	*Bundessocialhilfegesetz* (Germany)
ECHP	European Community Household Panel
EU	European Union
FAS	Training and Employment Activity
GMI	Guaranteed minimum income
JSA	Jobseeker's Allowance (UK)
NDYP	New Deal for Young People
NDLTU	New Deal for Long-term Unemployed
OECD	Organisation for Economic Co-operation and Development
PES	Public Employment Service
QCA	Qualitative comparative analysis
RMG	*Rendimento Mínimo Garantido* (Portugal)
RMI	*Revenu Minimum d'Insertion* (France)
SB	*Social bistand* (Denmark)
SWA	Supplementary Welfare Allowance (Ireland)
TANF	Temporary Assistance for Needy Families (USA)
TTK	*Toimeentulotuki* (Finland)
URC	Unemployment reintegration capacity
WIN	Work incentive
WIW	Jobseekers Employment Act

Acknowledgements

The contents of this book are extracted from the doctoral thesis I completed at the University of Bath (UK). Therefore I would like to express my gratitude to my supervisors, Dr Theodoros Papadopoulos and Professor Graham Room, for their patience, incentive, constructive criticism and support during its completion.

I would also like to thank Dr Philippe Van Kern and Professor Jos Berghman, at CEPS/INSTEAD (Luxembourg), for granting me access to the ECHP data, which was vital for the completion of this book. In addition, I would like to thank those who, through their constructive comments, in some way made a significant contribution to the completion of this study. In particular I would like to thank Dr Stuart White (Jesus College, University of Oxford, UK), who kindly accepted to participate in a seminar to discuss the content of the normative framework I put forward in this book. Also, I would like to thank Professor Ivar Lødemel (Oslo University College, Norway), for his valuable comments to the final draft of this book.

Finally, I would like to thank the Fundação para a Ciência e Teconologia (the Foundation for Science and Technology) in Portugal, for sponsoring the PhD degree that made this book possible.

ONE

Introduction

Minimum income schemes occupy a pivotal role in the overall architecture of social protection systems in Europe and other advanced economies. Commonly referred to as (general) social assistance (see Eardley et al, 1996a, p 28), or as safety-nets (Cox, 1998, p 397), these schemes provide the ultimate layer of income protection for those in need. They are the most evident expression of a societal commitment that all individuals are entitled to a dignified existence and that no one should experience unwanted need.

For the sake of clarity, minimum income schemes can be defined as schemes that provide a financial safety-net for individuals whose personal/household income is below the national social minimum. Because of their subsidiary nature, minimum income schemes are only available to individuals who (with some exceptions, such as family benefits) are no longer eligible for other forms of income protection. Unlike categorical social assistance, minimum income schemes are (quasi)universal, that is, they are not targeted at particular groups or social risks (Eardley et al, 1996a, p 28). Unlike social insurance, which provides insurance-based protection against (work-related) social risks, such as unemployment, old age or illness, minimum income schemes are a non-contributory form of protection (Lødemel and Schulte, 1992, pp 8-9). Currently, this serves to identify a number of schemes in Europe (see Table 1.1).

Minimum income schemes and the provision of a safety-net in Europe

There have been a number of attempts to map the differences in the provision of a minimum income in Europe.[1] The most comprehensive of these studies was carried out by Eardley et al (1996a), which identified five different clusters in the provision of social assistance in Europe (Eardley et al, 1996a, p 165) (see Table 1.2).[2] Despite its relevance, this study provides little information on the role of minimum income schemes in the broader framework of welfare provision. In light of this, it might be helpful to overlap it with the welfare state typology proposed by Ferrera and colleagues (2000).[3] Looking at aspects such as risk coverage and eligibility, the structure of benefits, the financing mechanisms and the organisational arrangements in place, the authors identify four welfare state models: the Scandinavian model, the Anglo-Saxon model, the Continental model and the South European model (Ferrera et al, 2000, pp 15-19) (see Table 1.3, page 10).

As can be seen in Table 1.3, in the Scandinavian and Anglo-Saxon models, minimum income schemes occupy a very specific and consistent function in the overall model of welfare provision. In the Scandinavian model – which includes

Table 1.1: Minimum income schemes in EU member countries (2007)

Country	Minimum income scheme	Country	Minimum income scheme
Austria	Sozialhilfe (social assistance)	Ireland	Supplementary Welfare Allowance
Belgium	Revenu d'Intégration/ Leefloon (social insertion income)	Luxembourg	Revenu Minimum Garanti (guaranteed minimum income)
Denmark	Kontanthjælp (social assistance)	Netherlands	Algemeine Bijstand (social assistance)
Finland	Toimeentulotuki (social assistance)	Portugal	Rendimento Social de Inserção (social insertion income)
France	Revenu Minimum d'Insertion (social insertion income)	Sweden	Ekonomiskt Bistånd (social assistance)
Germany	Arbeitslosengeld II, Sozialhilfe (social assistance)	Spain	Rentas Minimas (regional benefits)
Italy	Reddito Minimo d'Inserimento (social insertion income)	UK	Jobseeker's Allowance (non-contributory), Income Support

Sweden, Denmark and Finland – social security provides quasi-universal risk coverage and very generous social benefits. There is also a strong emphasis on active labour market policies (ALMP) and public social services (namely, childcare), with the purpose of increasing participation in the labour market. In light of this, minimum income schemes play only a marginal role in welfare provision. In addition, there is a significant level of local discretion in the delivery of the schemes, as implementation is the responsibility of local municipalities (Eardley et al, 1996a, pp 168-71; Ferrera et al, 2000, pp 15-19).

The Anglo-Saxon model is characterised by significant gaps in entitlement to social insurance. With the exception of healthcare, there is no universal coverage of social risks. Inactive people and those earning below a given threshold are not entitled to National Insurance benefits. In turn, there is a fairly integrated safety-net which, in light of the gaps in social insurance, covers a significant percentage of the population (see Eardley et al, 1996a, pp 168-71; Ferrera et al, 2000, pp 21-6).

There are significant differences in the provision of a minimum income guarantee in Continental countries. With the exception of the Netherlands, where

Table 1.2: Overlap of welfare state and social assistance typologies

Ferrera et al welfare state models	Eardley et al social assistance clusters				
	Welfare states with integrated safety-nets	Dual social assistance	Citizenship-based but residual assistance	Rudimentary assistance	Decentralised discretionary regime
Scandinavian			Sweden, Denmark, Finland		
Anglo-Saxon	UK (Ireland[4])				
Continental	Germany	France, Belgium, Luxembourg	The Netherlands		Austria
Southern Europe				Italy, Spain, Portugal and Greece	

Source: based on Eardley et al (1996a, pp 168-71); Ferrera et al (2000, pp 15-37)

some universal basic pensions schemes have been introduced, all these countries link the funding and delivery of social protection to the work status of individuals. Given its occupational basis, the social insurance system provides inclusive, but fragmented, coverage. Although, by and large, benefits are fairly generous, the relevance of minimum income schemes in the provision of social protection varies significantly. For instance, in the Netherlands and Austria, these schemes play a residual role in the protection of people in need. However, while in the former the right to minimum income protection is well established, in the latter this is subject to significant discretion by local authorities. In Germany, on the other hand, the social assistance scheme provides an integrated safety-net for those who trickle down the social security benefit structure. In France, Belgium and Luxembourg the provision of a safety-net to those in need is achieved through a (quasi)universal minimum income scheme, which is complemented by a number of targeted non-contributory schemes (Eardley et al, 1996a, pp 168-71; Ferrera et al, 2000, pp 26-31).

The Southern European model deserves special attention, as there have been significant changes in the provision of a minimum income since the study developed by Eardley et al (1996a, 1996b) was published. Before 1996, partly due to the significant reliance on the family in the provision of welfare, there were significant gaps in the framework of social protection in Southern European countries. Below the network of insurance-based income protection schemes, there was no unified safety-net to protect those in need. Only older people or those with disabilities were entitled to minimum income protection. In parallel, there was a number of discretionary programmes run by municipalities or charities (Eardley et al, 1996a, pp 168-71; Ferrera et al, 2000, pp 31-7). However, since then both Portugal and Italy have introduced (quasi)universal minimum income schemes. For instance, in 1996, Portugal introduced the *Rendimento Mínimo Garantido* (RMG), which was very much inspired by the French *Revenu Minimum d'Insertion* (RMI). Later, in 1998, the Italian government introduced (on an experimental basis) the *Reddito Minimo d'Inserimento*, which was supposed to create the basis for a more integrated safety-net (see Matsaganis et al, 2003). To a certain point, this reinforces the similarities of the model of social protection in these countries to that adopted in the Continental model of social protection.

From safety-net to trampoline

While originally focused on the provision of income security to those in need, the past two decades have been marked by a number of reforms that changed the mission and objectives of minimum income schemes in Europe. Although one cannot ignore the influence of the political debates and policy developments from across the Atlantic, the main factor that triggered this process was the substantial increase of unemployment. As Figure 1.1 illustrates, one of the consequences of this was the increase of the number of people depending on minimum income benefits, in particular between 1980 and 1990.

However, as Ferrera and Rhodes show (2000, pp 258-60), the increase in trade competition (which compelled governments to reduce the tax burden on business), the integration of financial markets (which forced governments to focus on the stability of inflation and interest rates), and the growing weight of healthcare and pensions systems in social expenditure, limited the ability of national governments to engage in expansionary policies to reduce unemployment and welfare caseloads. In light of this, there was a demand from different quarters for the need to activate minimum income recipients as a means to improve the employment effectiveness of income support schemes. For instance, the OECD's (Organisation for Economic Co-operation and Development) Jobs Study initiative, published in 1992, advocated that long-term assistance benefits should be made conditional on participation in active labour market programmes (OECD, 1994, pp 38-9). In the same year, the European Council suggested that, in order to improve the reintegration capacity of minimum income schemes, the right to a minimum income should be made conditional on a work requirement for able-bodied people. At the same time, member states were encouraged to offer training courses to help recipients return to the labour market (European Council, 1992, p 3).

In this context, a number of EU member countries introduced reforms aimed at activating minimum income recipients. In 1995 the UK government introduced

Figure 1.1: Recipient rates of lone-parent and social assistance benefits, as a percentage of the working-age population, in OECD member countries (1980, 1990 and 1999)

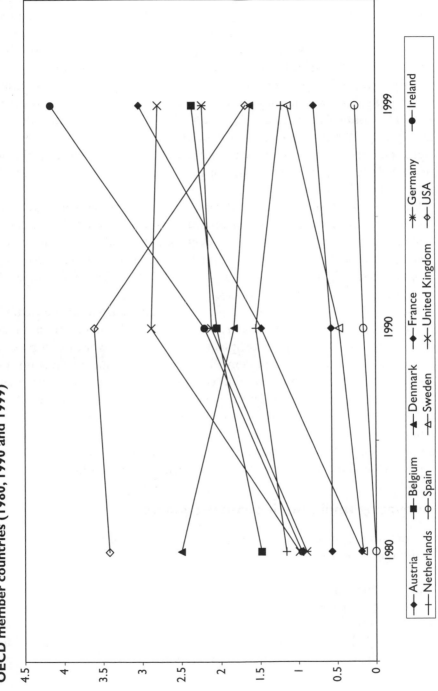

the Jobseekers Act, which made the receipt of benefit dependent on searching, and accepting, available jobs. Later, the government introduced New Deal programmes that provided work and training opportunities for unemployed people (Trickey and Walker, 2001, pp 186-92). In Sweden, the new Social Service Act of 1998 established that the right to social assistance for individuals aged between 20 and 24 was conditional on their participation in local labour market programmes or local activity programmes (see Salonen and Johansson, 1999, pp 11-12).

In Denmark, the law that regulated the provision of social assistance was amended in 1991 in order to compel municipalities to provide unemployed recipients under the age of 25 with advice and activation offers, such as subsidised job training, employment projects or education courses. This law was amended in 1993 in order to extend the activation offer to individuals above the age of 25 (Torfing, 1999, p 16). In 1998, the Act of Active Social Policy introduced a right and duty to activation. This meant the obligation to accept a suitable work offer, as defined by local authorities, or to participate in activation programmes (Rosdahl and Weise, 2001, p 167).

Finally, France, Spain, Portugal and Italy introduced minimum income schemes where the right to a minimum income was made conditional on individuals' willingness to engage in an insertion process, which could encompass active job-search, participation in education/training courses, participation in community programmes, and so on (Capucha, 1998, pp 30, 36-42; Enjolras et al, 2001, pp 50-2; Matsaganis et al, 2003, p 646).

As can be seen, these reforms imply a substantial change in the nature and objectives of minimum income schemes. First, the right to a minimum income was made conditional on the recipients' willingness to work or to participate in activation programmes. Entitlement to a minimum income was no longer dependent on lack of monetary resources alone, but on a visible commitment to engage in a process that would lead the recipient to become self-sufficient. Second, there is a greater emphasis on the reintegrative function of minimum income schemes. As Robert Henry Cox adequately puts its, the safety-net is replaced by a trampoline (1998, p 5). This implied greater attention on services offered to recipients with the view of assisting them back into the labour market.

Activating minimum income recipients

In order to fully understand the impact of activation on the role and nature of minimum income schemes, it is necessary to look more closely at how this has been implemented. But first, it is necessary to clarify precisely what activation means. Unfortunately, there are significant problems to this. First of all, the literature on this topic is populated by a number of overlapping concepts such as workfare (Lødemel and Trickey, 2001), welfare-to-work (Evans, 2001), ALMP (Martin, 1998) or the work approach (Hvinden, 1994), which make it difficult to define the conceptual frontiers of the notion of activation.

Second, and most importantly, there is little agreement as to the precise meaning of activation. For instance, according to Hanesh and Baltzer (2001), activation refers to '… a set of policies/measures/instruments aimed at integrating unemployed social assistance recipients into the labour market and improving their economic and social inclusion' (Hanesh and Baltzer, 2001, p 3). As the authors point out, activation involves a number of policy instruments – such as legislation, financial incentives and social or labour market services – that intervene in both the supply and demand sides of the labour market.

Hvinden (1999), on the other hand, sees activation as a set of policies aimed at reintegrating unemployed people in the labour market. He goes on to distinguish between a narrow and a wider approach to activation. The first refers to a set of policies that seek to promote participation in the primary labour market through increased job-search assistance, training and education, or job creation programmes. The second is focused on the personal development of individuals and involves participation in a wider set of activities such as protected labour markets, voluntary or community activities (Hvinden, 1999, p 28).

To a certain extent, this lack of consensus can be explained by the fact that the concept of activation has diverse meanings in different areas of public policy. For instance, in the employment area, activation refers to a more personalised treatment of jobseekers and the introduction of in-work benefits. In socio-cultural work, on the other hand, activation refers to a set of techniques and methodologies – which encompass reducing personal feelings of inferiority and insecurity, helping to establish individual objectives and to assume personal and social responsibilities – aimed at empowering individuals (Geldof, 1999, p 16).

In addition to this, there is significant variation in how activation has been implemented. For instance, while in most countries, the focus tends to be on a (more or less) swift return of minimum income recipients to the labour market, and off welfare, in France and Portugal, labour market integration is seen as only part of a broader strategy to promote the social insertion of minimum income recipients (see Guibentif and Bouget, 1997, pp 14-18).

Also, whereas in the majority of countries the option is to combine income support with a block of services and programmes designed to help recipients to return to the labour market, in other countries– in what Lødemel and Trickey call 'work instead of benefit policies' (2001, p xv) – the option is to replace the right to minimum income protection by the right to participate in a job creation scheme that provides individuals with an adequate level of income (see Guibentif and Bouget, 1997, pp 14-18; van Berkel and Møller, 2002, p. 50). A good example of this is France, where individuals aged under 25, with no children, are not entitled to *Revenu Minimum d'Insertion* (RMI), but are eligible to participate in Emploi Jeunes (Jobs For The Young), a programme that creates real-wage 'social utility activity' jobs that can last for up to five years (Enjolras et al, 2001, pp 61-64)

Reflecting on the previous paragraphs it is possible to identify what are the core issues that should be taken in consideration while circumscribing the notion of activation. Firstly, we need to determine what the main objective of activation is.

As seen earlier, the ultimate purpose of activation is to help recipients to become self-sufficient, and therefore to get them out of welfare. Although some countries (such as France or Portugal) adopt a broader understanding of how this can be accomplish, the common assumption underlying activation policies is that paid employment is the most effective way by which individuals can become self-sufficient.

Second, as the comparison between the conceptions put forward by Hanesh and Baltzer (2001) and Hvinden (1999) highlights, we need to identify which group(s) is (are) targeted by activation. Here we should clarify that, although the same policy can be applied to those receiving other types of income support (such as, unemployment or disability benefits), activation here applies only to (able-bodied) persons receiving minimum income benefits. Another issue that needs to be clarified, concerns the impact of activation on the individual's right to a minimum income. As seen earlier, activation involves a redefinition of the terms in which the right to a minimum income is defined. This entitlement is no longer dependent on the individuals' financial need alone, but also on their commitment to take the necessary actions to achieve their self-sufficiency.

Finally, as Hanesh and Baltzer (2001) conception of activation suggests, we need to circumscribe the policy instruments/tools used in the activation of minimum income recipients. As mentioned earlier, activation involves interventions in both the demand and the supply side of the labour market (Hanesh and Baltzer, 2001, p 3). However, more than identifying the type of intervention, the relevant question here is to access the nature of those interventions. As Guibentif and Bouget rightly put it, activation involves both negative and positive incentives (1997, pp 14-16). Therefore, activation cannot be solely identified by the introduction of work requirements and sanctions. It also incorporates a number of services, work and training opportunities designed to help individuals to become self-sufficient.

With this in mind, we can define activation as a policy of combining negative and positive incentives with the purpose of helping minimum income recipients to become self-sufficient through paid employment. However, if this conceptual exercise is to be successful, it is not sufficient to state the concept of activation that will be used throughout this book. This should be further confronted with two of the most relevant neighbouring concepts in the literature: workfare[5] and ALMP.

According to Lødemel and Trickey (2001), workfare refers to 'programmes or schemes that require people to work in return for social assistance benefits' (2001, p 6). As with activation, workfare is primarily about work. The purpose is that individuals become self-sufficient through (unsubsidised) paid employment or, if that is not possible, they participate in public work schemes in exchange for benefit (see Lødemel and Trickey, 2001, pp 8-9).

There are, nonetheless, some noticeable differences. First of all, the notion of workfare is geographically and historically bounded. It reverts to the introduction of work requirements into social assistance schemes in the United States, in the early 1970s (Hvinden, 1999, pp 28-9). Another difference lies in the fact that, although the 1996 reforms have introduced a broader range of work and training programmes for social assistance recipients – in what Nathan (1983) describes as 'new-style workfare' (see see Lødemel and Trickey, 2001, pp 4) – workfare, with its focus on work requirements, sanctions and time limits, has a fundamentally compulsive nature. This contradicts the focus on the combination of positive and negative incentives characteristic of activation (see Lødemel and Trickey, 2001, pp 7-8).

In the same way, this notion of activation should not be confused with the concept of ALMP. This notion is generally used to identify a series of labour market programmes that are aimed at the reduction of unemployment or other structural imbalnces in the labour market, such as promoting the labour market participation of women, promoting equal opportunities for people with disabilities or the economic recovery of specific regions or industries (Hvinden, 1999, pp 28-9; Kildal, 2000, p 5). In this sense, ALMP are part of the policy-mix used in the activation of minimum income. However, as they have no implication on the rules that define the entitlement to minimum income, ALMP cannot be confused with activation as a policy concept.

The conceptual clarification of the notion of activation cannot be completed without specifying how this concept treats programmes based on a 'work instead of benefit' approach. Bearing in mind that the explicit link between activation and the right to a minimum income, the notion of activation cannot cover those situations where the right to a minimum income is replaced by the right to participate in some kind of job creation programme.

Activation tools

As mentioned earlier, activation involves the use of positive and negative incentives. However, as Hanesh and Baltzer point out (2001, p 4), we should bear in mind that these incentives can be targeted at both the demand and the supply side of the labour market. In light of this, we can map the different activation incentives in the following way (see Table 1.3).

The introduction of activation requirements is a key component in the activation of minimum income recipients. As seen earlier, this activation requirement is expressed in two distinct formulae. In the first, which is the most common, the main purpose of activation is to find a job. The activation requirement is expressed as an obligation of active job-search, or mandatory enrolment in public employment services. Although this is mandatory to all able-bodied individuals, countries do consider some exceptions for individuals with childcare responsibilities, or with dependent adults in the family. In the second formula, the social insertion model, the main objective is to engage recipients in a multi-level strategy that is intended to reverse their situation. In this sense, the search for a job has the same priority as recovering from health problems, finding suitable accommodation, and so on (Guibentif and Bouget, 1997, pp 14-18).

Table 1.3: Positive and negative incentives used in the activation of minimum income recipients

	Supply-side interventions	Demand-side interventions
Negative incentives	Activation requirements (work tests) Insertion contracts Sanctions Time limits Reduction/curb on growth of cash benefits	
Positive incentives	Job-search assistance programmes (counselling, job-search support and training) Training Incentives or subsidies to individuals	State obligation to provide activation offers Incentives or subsidies for employers Job creation schemes (traditional job creation, intermediate labour market initiatives) Job sharing/job rotation

Source: Based on Hanesh and Baltzer (2001, p 4)

The enforcement of activation requirements is done with the help of sanctions. These can range from the termination of benefit entitlement, to partial cuts, or the temporary suspension of benefit. Some countries have a fixed-penalty regime, while others use progressive sanctions (see Eardley et al, 1996a, pp 149-52; Trickey, 2001, pp 276-7). In the US, some states have also introduced time limits on entitlement to social assistance (Bloom and Michalopoulos, 2001, pp 37-8). This has not been the case in Europe, however (Guibentif and Bouget, 1997, pp 31-2).

Reflecting the literature on unemployment traps in income support schemes which argues that the combined effect of high benefit rates and the taxation of incomes from work reduces the financial incentive for unemployed recipients to move to paid employment (Carone et al, 2004, p 32), some governments took measures to reduce the level of social assistance benefit rates, as it was the case in Sweden and in Finland, or to curb the growth of benefit levels – this was the case of the Netherlands, where the link between wages and social assistance benefits was frozen for three years (Cantillon et al, 2004, pp 528-35; Heikkila and Keskitalo, 2000, p 10).

The activation of minimum income recipients also involves positive incentives, both at the demand and supply-side level. In certain cases, supply-side interventions are aimed at improving the recipients' employability. This is achieved mainly through job-search assistance programmes such as in-depth counselling, job-search training, job brokering services and job clubs, along with a variety of training programmes. In other cases these supply-side interventions are designed to increase the recipients' incentive to take on paid employment. This is the case of in-work benefits, back-to-work grants, support for job-search costs or start-up incentives (Meager and Evans, 1997, pp 9-10; Martin, 1998, p 18).

Demand-side interventions, on the other hand, are intended to create additional work opportunities for minimum income recipients. In most cases, the provision of employment opportunities is not seen as a state obligation, it depends on political decisions and the availability of resources. This not the case, however, of Denmark and Sweden. As mentioned earlier, Danish municipalities are required to provide unemployed social assistance recipients with advice, counselling and a range of activation programmes (Torfing, 1999, p 16). In Sweden, municipalities are obliged to offer an activity to every young unemployed person who has not received a job or active labour market programme offer in the first 90 days of her unemployment period (Salonen and Johansson, 1999, p 14).

Two main types of demand-side intervention can be identified: direct job creation schemes and incentives to employers. In job creation schemes it is possible to differentiate between traditional job creation programmes, which consist of large-scale initiatives allowing the creation of jobs in the public and non-profit sector, and intermediate labour market initiatives, such as insertion enterprises, which consist of small-scale, local initiatives aimed at creating employment for those 'hard to employ'. Incentives to employers include exemptions from social security contributions, wage subsidies (or a combination of the two) and job sharing/job rotation programmes (Meager and Evans, 1997, pp 8-9).

Mapping the activation of minimum income recipients

Given the variety of tools used in the activation of minimum income recipients, there have been some attempts to map how these tools are combined in different geographical contexts. For instance, the US-based literature tends to differentiate between 'human capital development' and 'labour market attachment' approaches.[6] In the latter, the objective is to get recipients back to work as soon as possible. Hence, the focus is on intensive job-search assistance programmes such as job clubs, intensive client counselling and self-esteem building. Some education and training is provided, but only to the hard-to-employ.

Human capital development-oriented schemes have more broad and long-term objectives. Their aim is to help recipients find more stable jobs, that can provide better pay and more prospects for personal development. Hence, the focus is on basic education, professional training, job placement assistance and work-related support services (childcare, healthcare or transportation). Furthermore, as the focus is on sustainable transitions to work, recipients have some leniency in the choice of jobs they are prepared to accept. For instance, in Portland (Oregon,

US) recipients are encouraged to select jobs that provide better wages and more possibilities for personal development (Theodore and Peck, 2000, pp 85-9).

In Europe, a study carried out by Lødemel and Trickey (2001) suggests that there is a relationship between the schemes' structure of implementation and their ideological underpinning[7] (Trickey 2001, p 279). According to the authors, it is possible to identify a set of centralised schemes – namely the Danish Activation Act, the Jobseeker's Employment Act for Young People in the Netherlands and the New Deal for Young People in the UK – which tend to be more integrative and to focus more on human resource development. Schemes in this 'European centralised programmes' cluster tend to emphasise the structural basis of social exclusion processes, and focus on individual rights and on demand-side interventions.

Decentralised schemes, as is the case of the Norwegian workfare programme, tend to be preventive and to put a greater emphasis on quick labour market attachment. They therefore tend for focus on reducing individual dependency on benefits, on individual responsibilities and on the use of supply-side measures (Trickey, 2001, pp 279-80). There are, nonetheless, limits to this idea. For instance, the French RMI and the Help Towards Work programmes in Germany combine a decentralised administrative framework with a strong integrative focus (2001, pp 275-6, 280).

Activation dilemma

The activation of minimum income recipients implied significant changes in the character and role of these schemes. More than just providing income security for those in need, minimum income schemes are now expected to provide a range of services that are intended to help individuals to become self-sufficient. As well as changes in the implementation and delivery of minimum income schemes, this has prompted two important, and complementary, debates.

The first concerns the terms in which one can justify the right to a minimum income. The introduction of activation requirements bears the crux of the problem. Does the activation requirement not undermine the dignity of the individuals that the right to a minimum income is supposed to protect? At the same time, shouldn't individuals be expected to contribute to a society which produces resources that guarantee their survival? Even if the latter premise is accepted, it is still necessary to determine what are the conditions are under which recipients should be asked to fulfil their obligations. For instance, is it fair to ask recipients to fulfil this requirement even if they do not have adequate opportunities to do so? Also, is work the only type of activity that can make a contribution to society?

The second debate concerns a balance between fairness and effectiveness. Previous sections have shown that, with the purpose of improving the employment effectiveness of minimum income schemes, a number of countries have taken measures that could be seen as putting at stake some basic individual rights. Nowhere is this more evident than in the policy adopted by Sweden or Finland to reduce benefit rates in minimum income schemes as a means of inducing people to get back into the labour market. The underlying assumption here is that the employment effectiveness of minimum income is contradictory to the requirement of treating recipients fairly. This raises the question of whether respecting the rights of minimum income recipients can hamper the employment effectiveness of the schemes.

This book will engage in debates prompted by the activation of minimum income recipients. The first part (Chapters Two and Three) determines how the right to a minimum income can be adequately justified. Chapter Two demonstrates that the arguments posed by Philippe Van Parijs (1997) and Mead (1986), which typify the fundamental standpoints in the literature, fail to provide an adequate justification of the right to a minimum income. Reflecting on the difficulties faced by Mead and Van Parijs, it is argued that a more satisfactory alternative is possible. This alternative can only be successful if it is set in the context of an ontological framework that focuses on promoting an individual's personal development, but recognises its social basis, and the obligations that this imposes, and encompasses a more critical view of the role of the market as a mechanism of social regulation.

Chapter Three then sets about developing a normative framework to provide an adequate justification of the right to a minimum income. Using the ontological frameworks proposed by Karl Marx and John Stuart Mill as terms of comparison, the first part of Chapter Three demonstrates that Durkheim's theory of social justice provides a theorisation of society, market and individual from which an adequate justification of the right to a minimum income can be derived. In line with Durkheim's theory of social justice. It is argued that each individual has a right to exploit her talents – a right to personal development – which can be exercised while performing a social function in society, such as paid employment, unpaid work in social economy organisations, providing care to dependent family members or improving her human capital through education or training. In order to secure this right, social actors and institutions must:

- meet the individual's basic consumption needs;
- eliminate direct and indirect constraints to the individual's choices on the best way to exploit its talents;
- provide individual's with opportunities to exploit its talents;
- enforce, through the use of restitutive sanctions, an individual's obligation to exploit its talents so as to enable the personal development of others.

The last section of Chapter Three shows that, as it recognises that the right to a minimum income should be made conditional on the fulfilment of a contribution requirement, that this requirement must be enforced in a context where individuals have the opportunity to fulfil their obligations, and that recognises the variety of activities that make a contribution to society, the right to personal development can provide an adequate justification of the right to a minimum income.

Having demonstrated that the right to personal development can provide an adequate justification for the right to a minimum income, this framework can then be used as the normative standpoint to analyse the balance between fairness and effectiveness in the activation of minimum income recipients. The second part of this book (Chapters Four to Seven) tests the hypothesis that, because they combine both positive and negative incentives, minimum income schemes that show more respect for the right to personal development, once labour market conditions are accounted for, are more effective at returning recipients to the labour market.

Chapter Four provides the methodological framework for the comparative study that is used to validate the hypothesis mentioned above. After a brief description of the cases under analysis, this chapter demonstrates that the relation between the employment effectiveness of minimum income schemes and their respect for the right to personal development can be best analysed by combining the heuristic potential of QCA (qualitative comparative analysis), simple correlational tools and cluster analysis.

The first moment of this comparative study consists in the measurement of the schemes' respect for the right to personal development. In line with this normative framework, Chapter Five measures to what degree the schemes provide recipients with an adequate level of income; how free they are to choose other activities instead of paid employment or the job they wish to perform; what is the level of discretion in the implementation of the schemes; what are the recipients' opportunities to work or to participate in education/training courses; and what is the character of the sanction regime they are subjected to.

After measuring the schemes' respect for the right to personal development, the next step is to measure their employment effectiveness. Chapter Six starts by looking at the percentage of recipients who, a year after being on minimum income, made a transition to unsubsidised work. However, bearing in mind that the differences between the cases under analysis could be affected by labour market conditions, it is argued that the employment effectiveness of minimum income schemes, should be measured through a marginal employment effectiveness indicator that can capture the ability of labour markets to create jobs for unemployed people – their unemployment reintegration capacity.

In line with the methodological framework defined earlier, Chapter Seven then uses QCA, simple correlational tools and cluster analysis to explore the relationship between the schemes' employment effectiveness and their respect for the right to personal development. This shows that, with the exception of the recipients' freedom to choose other activities besides paid employment, schemes can successfully combine respect for recipients' right to personal development with higher levels of employment effectiveness.

Having provided an answer to the questions posed by the activation of minimum income recipients, Chapter Eight then reviews the main contributions and discusses how these could be further elaborated in additional research.

Notes

[1] A first attempt to map the provision of the right to a minimum income in Europe, which focuses solely on (Western) Germany, the UK, the Netherlands, Belgium and France, was conducted by Milano (1989). A more comprehensive study was later conducted by Lødemel and Schulte (1992, pp 12-13, 18-19), who identified four poverty regimes: the institutionalised poverty regime, associated with the UK; the differentiated poverty regime, typical of corporatist welfare states such as France and Germany; the residual poverty regime, which incorporated Nordic countries; and the incomplete differentiated regimes type, which included Southern Europe countries (see Lødemel and Schulte, 1992, pp 12-13, 18-19).

[2] Ian Gough tried to confirm the validity of this typology by applying cluster analysis to the original data. Focusing on the level of generosity, inclusiveness and extensiveness of social assistance schemes, the author found that, where Europe was concerned, only two of the original regimes were confirmed: the citizenship-based but residual regime and the decentralised discretionary regime. The study also showed that there were significant differences within the Latin regime. According to Gough (2001, pp 168-9), while there are significant similarities between Portugal and Greece, Spain and Italy are closer to the Continental model.

[3] Despite its relevance for welfare state theory, Esping-Andersen's welfare regime typology (1990) does not provide the best option for this comparison. First of all, Esping-Andersen's initial typology does not differentiate the specificity of the social protection model adopted in Southern European countries. Second, Esping-Andersen's welfare-regime typology ignores the role of social assistance schemes in welfare provision (Esping-Andersen 1990, p. 54). Instead, Esping-Andersen uses the level of expenditure on general social assistance schemes as an indicator of the role of the welfare state as a system of stratification. More specifically, the author points to the salience of means-tested benefits and the relative weight of private provision of pensions and health-care as evidence of the centrality of the market as a principle of stratification in the liberal-regime cluster (Esping-Andersen, 1990, pp 61-5, 69-76).

[4] Curiously, the authors do not include Ireland in this model. Although they accept that it shares a number of characteristics with the British model, the authors argue that Ireland, with its focus on negotiated adjustment, has gradually diverged from it (see Ferrera et al, 2000, p 21). However, the authors fail to relocate Ireland in any other cluster.

[5] According to Kildal (2000), welfare-to-work is a mere variant of workfare. They both focus on the application of compulsory elements in benefits for the workless poor. However, welfare-to-work seems to provide more education and training opportunities, and better working conditions than workfare (2000, p 5).

[6] This is not the only typology available. For instance, in their review of US-based evidence, Bloom and Michalopoulos (2001, pp 10-11) identify four different approaches:

- job-search first approach
- education first approach
- employment-focused with mixed initial activities
- education-focused with mixed initial activities.

[7] This is not to ignore the existence of other relevant studies in this domain, such as Kildal's study of workfare schemes in Scandinavian countries (2000), or Handler's (2004) study of workfare programmes in Europe and the US.

TWO

The right to a minimum income: between Mead and Van Parijs

As seen in Chapter One, the introduction of activation requirements has generated a debate over the conditional nature of the right to a minimum income. Going through the literature, it can be observed that this debate crosses over various domains within political theory. This chapter will try to determine if the arguments presented by Mead and Van Parijs, who typify the fundamental standpoints in the literature on this topic, provide an adequate justification for the right to a minimum income.

The right to a minimum income in political theory

One of the domains within political theory that is relevant to the justification of the provision of the right to a minimum income is the set of theories that debate over principles that should regulate the functioning of political communities, more commonly referred to as theories of justice. This the case of Rawls' conception of 'justice as fairness', where the author tries to determine the principles that individuals would choose to govern the functioning of social institutions and the distribution of primary social goods, that is, all the means needed to pursue a given conception of a good life[1] (Rawls, 2001, p 35). First, Rawls states that each individual is entitled to exercise all equal basic liberties, such as freedom of conscience, freedom of expression, private property and due process of law liberty principle (2001, p 68). He then states that the distribution of social and economic inequalities must take place in a context where all positions in society are open to all citizens under fair equality of opportunity – the liberal equality principle – and in such a way that it privileges the least advantaged in a given community – the difference principle (Rawls, 2001, p 239). In light of this, it could be argued that the introduction of the right to a minimum income, in the sense that it guarantees a basic level of income that enables individuals to compete for a position in society, could be justified as a form of guaranteeing a fair equality of opportunity. In fact, as it is targeted as those most in need, a minimum income would also respect Rawls' principle of difference.[2]

Besides the principles that are expected to regulate the functioning of social institutions, Rawls' conception of justice as fairness also defines a number of principles that should guide the behaviour of individuals. One of these is the principle of fairness, which requires obedience to the rules of a (just) institution whenever an individual has voluntarily benefited from the rewards and opportunities produced by that institution. The underlying logic is that individuals should not take unfair advantage from the efforts made by others, without giving the fair share that is expected from them (Rawls, 2001, pp 267–8). In light of this, it could be argued that under Rawls' conception of justice as fairness the right to a minimum income should be made conditional on some kind of contribution requirement.

Gutmann and Thompson (1996) put forward a more explicit argument as to the conditional nature of the right to a minimum income. Their theory of deliberative democracy argues that conflicts over fundamental values should be resolved by reference to the principles of reciprocity, publicity and accountability. However, contrary to traditional deliberative theories, this is not a purely procedural framework. Thus, the deliberation process is regulated by three substantive principles:

- the principle of basic liberty, which secures individuals from violations of their physical and mental integrity;
- the principle of basic opportunity, which guarantees citizens access to the basic goods that secure a good life (such as healthcare, education, work and income);
- the principle of fair opportunity, which requires a merit-based distribution of certain goods in society (Muhlberger, 2000, p 7).

On the one hand, these substantive principles act as conditions to the deliberative process, in the sense that they limit the possibility of reaching resolutions that might violate the ideas of basic liberty or basic opportunity. On the other hand, they constitute the prerequisites of the whole deliberative process, as they guarantee the possibility of equal standing for all participants.

The provision of a right to a minimum income is one of the most obvious ways of realising the basic opportunity principle. However, the guarantee of a minimum income should respect the principle of reciprocity, which entails the idea of mutual dependence.[3] Given the fact that the resources that secure a minimum income guarantee are produced by those engaged in productive economic activity, then those who make a claim on those resources must be available to participate in the productive process that generates it, that is, they need to be available to work. But the principle of reciprocity also involves social responsibilities to society: '… citizens who need income support are obliged to work, but only if their fellow citizens fulfil their obligation to enact public policies that provide adequate employment and child support' (Gutmann and Thompson, 1996, p 276).

The relevance of the previous arguments should not give the impression that the existence of the right to a minimum income is consensual in this particular domain of political theory. Robert Nozick's entitlement theory, for instance, challenges the legitimacy of distributive policies such as the provision of right to a minimum income. In contrast with 'end state' theories, where social justice is evaluated in terms of its distributive consequences, Nozick departs from the assumption that individuals hold a number of inviolable rights (entitlements), and that a situation is deemed just when it derives from the exercise of those rights, and unjust when it involves their violation. From this point of view, any inequalities that do not derive from the violation of individuals' rights are just, even if those in the more advantageous positions do not merit them. Consequently, any attempt to reduce just inequalities, such as the establishment of a right to a minimum income, would be unjust (Fitzpatrick, 2001, pp 45-6).

Theories of social justice and the right to a minimum income

The issue of the right to a minimum income has gained particular relevance in the context of the debate over the notion of social justice. This is in great part due to the impact of Van Parijs' proposal of a basic income. The author argues that a just society must maximise 'real freedom', that is, the freedom to do whatever one might want to do (1997, p 23). The main institutional implication of achieving a just society would be the introduction of an unconditional basic income, bestowed regardless of a person's income, place of residence, household situation, and most importantly, her willingness to work (Van Parijs, 1997, pp 30-3).

Van Parijs' proposal prompted a number of counterarguments that claim that the distribution of resources in society should respect the notion of reciprocity. This is the case of Stuart White's civic minimum (2003), which consists of a series of policies and institutions that would satisfy the demands of (non-ideal) fair reciprocity. According to White (2003, p 19) this requires:

- that no person suffers poverty of income due to forces beyond their control (non-immiseration);
- adequate protection against market vulnerability and associated risks of exploitation and abuse (market security);
- adequate opportunity for self-realisation in work (work as a challenge);
- minimisation of class inequality, that is, the reduction of inequalities in initial endowments of wealth and educational opportunity to a reasonable minimum.

When a society fulfils these requirements, an individual who claims a generous share of the social product has an obligation to make an adequate productive contribution to the community – the basic work expectation (White, 2003, p 96). This consists of performing a number of hours of civic labour, which comprises all forms of labour that provide a significant service for, or on behalf of, the wider community, be it paid employment (both market and non-market based), parental care, care of the infirm or household work (White, 2003, pp 98-112).

Another interesting stream in this debate can be found in the set of theories that try to define the fundamental premises of the idea of human well-being (see Clark and McGillivray, 2007, p 1). One relevant standpoint in this domain is Doyal and Gough's 'theory of human needs' (1991). They start from the premise that in order to avoid serious harm, here seen as a dramatically impaired participation in a form of life, individuals have two basic needs: physical health and autonomy (1991, p 55). Although the mode of satisfaction of these needs varies from culture to culture, Doyal and Gough argue that it is possible to identify a number of common characteristics in the goods or services necessary for the enhancement of the health and autonomy of individuals. These properties, which Doyal and Gough define as intermediate needs, can be seen as second-order goals necessary for the full satisfaction of the needs of individuals. The list of intermediate needs includes: nutritional food and clean water; protective housing; a non-hazardous work environment; a non-hazardous physical environment; appropriate healthcare; security in childhood; physical security; appropriate education; safe birth control and childbearing; and economic security (Doyal and Gough, 1991, pp 157-8).

Doyal and Gough's (1991) stance on the legitimacy of a right to a minimum income, and on its conditional nature, can be found in their discussion of the right to need satisfaction. Doyal and Gough accept that social life depends on the fulfilment of our individual obligations towards others. However, unless the individuals' minimal levels of need are satisfied they cannot be expected to be able to fulfil those obligations (see Doyal and Gough, 1991, pp 93-99). This creates an entitlement, a right, to need satisfaction. So, it seems plausible to argue that under Doyal and Gough's normative, we can justify the provision of a minimum income as a means of satisfying the need of individuals for economic security (see Doyal and Gough, 1991, pp 92-96).

Although the authors fail to discuss the issue of conditionality per se, there are reasons to believe Doyal and Gough's reciprocal conception of the relation between rights and duties would justify the introduction of an activation requirement in the entitlement to a minimum income. In fact, they even admit the possibility that '… individuals who refuse to act in accordance with this reciprocity (e.g. criminals) may lose entitlements that others do not' (Doyal and Gough, 1991, p 93).

Sen's 'capability approach' (2001) provides an interesting alternative to the argument put forward by Doyal and Gough (1991). Sen argues that inequality should be examined in terms of the ability of individuals to achieve valuable functionings, that is the things a person might value doing or being. A person's 'capability' refers to the combination of functionings that are possible for a person to achieve, that is, the freedom to achieve different lifestyles (2001, p 75). Despite its comprehensiveness, Sen's capability approach does not discuss the right to a minimum income per se. Nonetheless, Sen's stance on the issue can be inferred from his analysis of the relationship between poverty and capabilities, and between capabilities and rights. He argues that poverty should be viewed not in terms of lack of income, but in terms of the deprivation of basic capabilities,[4] that is the inability to satisfy the fundamental functionings of individuals (Sen, 1993, p 41; 2001, pp 87-90). Rather than writing off the role of income in the analysis of poverty, Sen's main purpose is to emphasise its instrumental character with regards to capabilities. He goes on to suggest that '… as long as minimal capabilities can be achieved by enhancing the income level […] it will be possible […] to identify the minimally adequate income for reaching the minimally acceptable capability levels' (1993, p 42).

Bearing in mind the fact that, according to Sen (1981, p 16), it is possible to derive a theory of rights from his capability approach (the 'capability rights system'), it could be argued that the right to a minimum income can be justified in order to secure a minimum level of capability to individuals. However, contrary to Doyal and Gough (1991), Sen's conception of rights does not entail any reciprocity requirements. Accepting that in some cases the connection between rights and duties deserves some merit, rights should be seen as entitlements shared by all, irrespective of citizenship (1999, p 230). Therefore, under Sen's normative framework, the right to a minimum income could not be made conditional on some kind of activation requirement.

Welfare theory and the right to a minimum income

The debate over the right to a minimum income is intrinsic to the discussion of social rights, and on their conditional nature. According to Marshall, social rights can go from '... the right to a modicum of economic welfare and security to the right to share to the full in the social heritage and to live the life of a civilised being according to the standards prevailing in society' (Marshall and Bottomore, 1992, p 8). Nevertheless, Marshall recognises that social rights are conditional on the fulfilment of the duties of citizenship (Marshall and Bottomore, 1992, p 26). These encompass both a general obligation '... to live the life of a good citizen, giving such service as one can to promote the welfare of the community' (1992, p 26), and more precise obligations, such as the duty to pay taxes and insurance contributions, to become educated or to perform military service.

However, Marshall is ambiguous about the fairness of making the right to income support – where the right to a minimum income is included – conditional on the exercise of a duty to work. On the one hand, this would undermine the role of social rights in reducing the level of market-induced inequalities. On the other hand, Marshall recognises that this is legitimate if the economic situation requires it. However, he points out that the constitution of large national communities – where responsibilities become more diffuse – and the availability of jobs guaranteed by full employment policies, have actually weakened this obligation. As he puts it '... the essential duty is not to have a job and hold it, since that is relatively simple in conditions of full employment, but to put one's heart into one's job and work hard' (Marshall and Bottomore, 1992, pp 45-6).

In contrast to Marshall, Titmuss is clearly hostile to the idea of making the right to a minimum income conditional on the exercise of the duty to work. This is clear from his criticism of the Victorian Poor Law. According to Titmuss (Deacon, 2002, p 17), these made the redistribution of resources conditional on a number of moral judgements on people in need and their behaviour, hence harming their sense of self-respect and self-determination: 'Within the established pattern of commonly held values, the system could only be redistributive by being discriminatory and socially divisive' (Titmuss, 2001, pp 104-5). Therefore, only universal social rights would be able to redistribute social resources without discriminating between individuals. Dahrendorf provides an additional argument against the introduction of work requirements. From his point of view (Dahrendorf, 1996, pp 32-3), citizenship rights are based on a social contract valid for all members in society. Work, on the other hand, is a private contract. Consequently, if rights are made dependent on people entering into private employment relations, this destroys the voluntary character of the employment relation, which amounts to forced work.

This idea of the unconditional nature of social rights has been contested by a number of authors, in particular those identified with the communitarian school of thought. A good example of this is Selbourne's *The principle of duty* (1997). The principle of duty is the founding principle of the civic order, a metaphor for a morally integrated community/society. According to Selbourne (1997, pp 141, 143-5), the state-based, universalistic, provision of welfare services (which were previously provisioned on the basis of personal obligation) has undermined the principle of duty. The restoration of the civic order would require the strengthening and enforcement of the principle of duty. In particular, he argues that the abuse or misuse of welfare benefits should be sanctioned. For instance, individuals who refuse training or work offers should be faced with the loss or curtailment of their unemployment benefits (Selbourne, 1997, pp 292-3).

Another example of this communitarian line of argument can be found in Mead's argument of the introduction of work requirement in welfare programmes. Mead claims that traditional welfare programmes have failed to develop the ability of individuals to function in society (1986, pp 61-7). In light of this, he argues that government programmes should enforce the obligations of individuals. More specifically, the right to a minimum income should be made conditional on the obligation to perform/search for work (1986, pp 167-8).

In the same way as Mead or Selbourne, Amitai Etzioni calls for a rebalance between rights and responsibilities as part of a broader agenda concerned with the moral revival of modern communities. According to Etzioni (1994, pp 263-4), the provision of welfare services should be shaped by the principle of reciprocity. Individuals are expected to provide for themselves and their families through paid employment. On the other hand, the community is responsible for providing the basic needs of those who truly cannot provide for themselves. Despite his emphasis on the responsibilities of individuals, Etzioni stresses the centrality of a minimum income guarantee – or social basics – as the foundation of a good society. Furthermore, in contrast with Mead, Etzioni argues that public funds should be used to create community jobs that would allow individuals to fulfil their responsibility to support themselves (1997, pp 82-3).

The idea of conditioning the exercise of social rights has also been advocated by other authors, outside the communitarian school. Pierre Rosanvallon and Jean-Paul Fitoussi argue that the growth of new forms of social exclusion and the financing problems of the welfare state require a rearrangement of the relationship between rights and responsibilities. They propose a framework of citizenship rights based on liberty rights, which combine Marshall's civil and political rights; credit rights, which comprise traditional passive social rights; and integration rights, which embody a new set of social rights that entail a reciprocal relation between the individual and society (Rosanvallon, 1995, pp 138-40). According to Rosanvallon and Fitoussi, the insertion policies introduced in France in the early 1990s, as they established links between moral obligations and welfare provision, and explored new forms of public employment creation, reflect this new conception of social citizenship (Rosanvallon and Fitoussi, 1997, p 166).

Anthony Giddens provides a more wide-ranging argument on the need to make some social rights dependent on the fulfilment of individual responsibilities. According to Giddens (1999, pp 4, 7), the rise of a risk society undermines the insurance logic that underlies the welfare state that emerged from the post-Second World War. Whereas unconditional rights are adequate to deal with external risks – that is, risks that are regular enough and can easily be protected through public insurance – they are inadequate to deal with manufactured risks – that is, risks that are produced by the progress of science and technology and are difficult to predict and to insure. This opens the way for a redefinition of individual and social responsibilities, where individuals are called to a more active management of their material and social conditions. Therefore, Giddens argues, it is necessary to connect rights with responsibilities.

Mapping the debate on the right to a minimum income

As the previous section has shown, the debate over the right to a minimum income traverses various domains within political theory. In fact, there are significant commonalities between the standpoints revised earlier. For instance, as the work of Gutmann and Thompson, White or Etzioni shows, the notion of reciprocity is used within different domains of political theory. Also, Van Parijs' proposal for a basic income has gone outside the realm of social justice theory, and gained great relevance in the debate over the nature of the social rights of citizenship (see Plant, 2004). It is possible therefore to identify a number of core issues that structure the debate over the right to a minimum.

The central issue concerns the conditional nature of the right to a minimum income. For some, such as Van Parijs, Sen or Titmuss, the right to a minimum income cannot be made conditional on any kind of work or activation requirement. As other social rights, this is supposed to offset inequalities generated by the market and to allow individuals to choose freely how to lead their lives. However, a large number of authors – from Gutmann and Thompson, to White or Mead – would argue that the right to a minimum income, as well as other social rights, presupposes the production of resources on a cooperative basis, which in turns requires individuals to make some kind of contribution in return for their benefit. For some, in particular Mead, Etzioni or Selbourne, the right to a minimum income is seen as a subsidiary form of protection to that provided by paid employment, which reinforces its conditional character.

The conditional character of the right to a minimum income entails two further issues. First, it is necessary to determine what the conditions are for the exercise of one's responsibilities. Some authors, such as Mead or Selbourne, prefer to stress the mandatory character of individual responsibilities. Others recognise that there is a clash between the notion of reciprocity and the equality of opportunities available to individuals. Stuart White's notion of fair reciprocity, for instance, departs from the idea that the enforcement of reciprocity as a distributive principle should acknowledge that it is unfair to force individuals to make a contribution to the community regardless of their effective opportunities or ability to contribute (White, 2003, pp 114–16). This idea is also present in Gutmann and Thompson's notion of fair workfare. They suggest that the obligation to look for a job needs to be balanced with the investment in childcare services that relieves lone mothers from their parental obligations (1996, p 290). Etzioni suggests that the enforcement of work requirements should be accompanied by the creation of community jobs that create real work opportunities for income support recipients (1997, p 82–3).

Besides the issue of what the conditions are for the exercise of personal responsibilities, it is also necessary to establish what can be considered as an appropriate form of contribution to society. As the previous section shows, some authors, such as Mead or Gutmann and Thompson, identify work as the main form of contribution to society. In contrast, there are others who argue that individuals can make a contribution to society in ways other than work. This is the case with Stuart White's notion of civic labour. According to White, civic labour includes any '... kind of work [that] is sufficiently valuable to other citizens to count in reciprocation for the goods and services they have supplied' (2003, p 99). Bearing in mind the importance of the market as a mechanism to determine the value citizens assign to a given good or service, the notion of civic labour points, in the first instance, to market-generated paid employment. However, civic labour also covers other valuable activities that are not produced through the market, such as in the case of work done in the production of public and merit goods[5] or care work performed within households (White 2003, pp 101–12).

Mead, Van Parijs and the right to a minimum income

The previous sections have shown, first, that the debate on the right to a minimum income traverses a number of domains within political theory, and, second, that the debate is organised around three main questions: can the right to a minimum income be made conditional on some kind of contribution requirement? What are the conditions for the exercise of one's responsibilities? And what can be considered as an appropriate form of contribution to society? The challenge now is to determine if any of the standpoints in the literature provide an adequate justification of the right to a minimum income.

Given the practical unfeasibility of making a fully fledged evaluation of all the various standpoints, the most adequate option seems to to restrict this exercise to two typical, indeed dominant, arguments in the literature: Van Parijs' argument for an unconditional basic income and Mead's argument for the introduction of work requirements (see Fitzpatrick, 2001; Lødemel and Trickey, 2001; Deacon, 2002; Standing, 2002). Hence, bearing in mind the questions mentioned earlier, the following sections try to determine if any of these authors can provide an adequate justification of the right to a minimum income.

Mead and the argument for the introduction of work requirements

According to Mead, the introduction of work requirements serves both the interest of the individuals and of the community. He views the role of social policy as an extension of the Hobbesian conception of the state: the maintenance of public order. Rather than just law and peacefulness, order here includes all the socially produced conditions necessary for people to have a satisfactory life (Mead, 1986, p 5). According to Mead, social order requires not only passive compliance, but also the fulfilment of the expectations other individuals have in relation to the public role an individual performs as a worker, a parent or a neighbour. The ability of individuals to function in society is related with their capacity to respond to these expectations (Mead, 1986, p 6; Deacon, 2002, p 51).

This conception of social order is well reflected in Mead's theory of citizenship. According to Mead, this involves both rights and duties. Hence, traditional social rights, which protect people against need, unemployment and other social risks, need to be matched by social obligations. Mead identifies five core common obligations to all individuals: work in available jobs, unless aged or disabled; supporting (as much as possible) one's family; fluency and literacy (in English); learning in order to become employable; and abiding by the law (Mead, 1986, p 242).

According to Mead, '... work for the employable is the clearest social obligation' (1986, p 243). This can be traced to the significance of the work ethic as a founding value of North American society. In fact, Mead argues, its importance has grown, as work and the workplace seem to be replacing other forms of communitarian existence such as ethnicity, religion or the family. This has specific implications for Mead's view of the conditional nature of the right to income support: '... while individuals make claims for sustenance through politics and their own labours, they must also contribute to a reservoir of resources, both economic and moral, shared by all citizens' (1986, p 246).

As mentioned earlier, the introduction of work requirements is not justified on the interest of the community alone, but on an individual's self-interest (1986, p 246). Based on his analysis of Work Incentive (WIN) programmes, he argues that the enforcement of work obligations is key to improving the employment effectiveness of income support programmes. According to Mead, these programmes traditionally tended to assume that, given the opportunity, individuals would fulfil their responsibilities – the competence assumption (Mead, 1997, p 13). However, the WIN experience showed that the more effective offices were those which had broader notions of employability, were more successful at transmitting to recipients that they were required to work, and were more willing to impose sanctions if necessary (Mead, 1986, pp 156-68).

Van Parijs and the right to a basic income

As mentioned earlier, Van Parijs argues that a free society is one that realises real freedom for all (1997, p 27). His notion of real freedom stands on three fundamental principles: that there is some well-enforced structure of rights (security); that this structure is such that each person owns herself (self-ownership); and, that each person has the greatest possible opportunity to do whatever she might want to do (leximin opportunity)[6] (Van Parijs 1997, p. 25). The main institutional implication of achieving a just society would be the introduction of an unconditional basic income, bestowed regardless of the individual's income, place of residence, household situation or willingness to work (1997, p 30). The significance of the basic income is not related with the possibility of equating everybody's wealth, or purchasing power; but with the possibility that people are able to choose between different goods or even different lifestyles[7] (Van Parijs, 1997, p 33; Gough, 2000, p 205).

While building his argument for an unconditional basic income, Van Parijs tries to rebut two challenges that share the same underlying idea: that the introduction of a basic income would unfairly favour those who are voluntarily unemployed. The first criticism is that an unconditional basic income would favour those with a preference for leisure against those who were keen to work more in order to achieve a higher income – the Crazy-Lazy dilemma (1997, p 93). Van Parijs argues that, in order to carry out its productive activities, Crazy uses more external resources than Lazy. Hence, giving Lazy a basic income that is funded by the taxation of the proceeds made by Crazy does not discriminate the latter. In fact, this resets the equal distribution of external resources and, consequently, leximins opportunity between Crazy and Lazy (Van Parijs, 1997, pp 92-102; Gough, 2000, p 208).

Van Parijs extends this line of thought when he argues that basic income should be funded through the taxation of employment rents. The author starts by arguing that, due to a combination of the effect of minimum wages, efficiency wages and high turnover costs, a large number of individuals are excluded from participation in the labour market. In light of this, jobs can be seen as external assets, the same as inherited wealth and skills. Therefore, each person who holds a job earns a particular employment rent, which is given by the difference of the income (and other advantages) a person gets from her job, and what she would get in a situation of a perfect labour market (Van Parijs, 1997, p 108). As a consequence, rather than favouring those who do not want to work, a basic income funded by the taxation of employment rents would reduce the inequality in the distribution of work-related assets (Van Parijs, 1997, pp 106-9).

Besides the charge that a basic income would unfairly favour the voluntarily unemployed, Van Parijs is also forced to consider the challenge that the introduction of a basic income would generate exploitative situations, that is, it would allow certain individuals to take an unfair advantage of someone else's work. In order to deal with this challenge, he considers different three interpretations of exploitation.[8] In a first stage, he considers the 'Lockean' conception of exploitation'. Underlying this conception is the idea that that a person is entitled to the total product of her labour (see Van Parijs, 1997, pp 145-50; White, 1997, p 323). Therefore, whenever someone '... appropriates, or jointly controls, part of the net product by virtue of something other than her labour contribution to it, this can be seen to create an exploitative situation' (Van Parijs, 1997, pp 145-46).

He then examines the 'Lutheran' conception of exploitation. Underlying this conception is the idea that a person is entitled to a share of the total product that is proportional to the value of her individual labour contribution. Therefore, there is exploitation whenever a someone appropriates, through her income, more than the labour value they have produced (see Van Parijs, 1997, pp 153; White, 1997, p 323). The third conception of exploitation analysed by Van Parijs conveys what White calls the 'strong effort' principle, which implies that a person's income should be strictly proportional to their work effort.[9] As a consequence, there is exploitation whenever the income a person receives is disproportional to the labour she has performed (see Van Parijs, 1997, pp 160-4; White, 1997, p 323)

Van Parijs accepts that, if judged by reference to any of these principles, the introduction of a basic income would generate exploitative situations (Van Parijs, 1997, pp 145-69; White, 1997, p 323). He argues, however, that these three conceptions might also generate brute luck inequalities in income – that is, inequalities that do not result from individual choices – which render them inconsistent with the principle of leximin opportunity. As an alternative, Van Parijs suggests that the relation between one's work and the ensuing proceeds should be governed by a 'weak effort' principle. This stipulates that there should be a positive correlation between one's work and the return it generates. In this case, the introduction of a basic income would not distress the positive correlation between contribution and return while improving a person's ability to choose the lifestyle she prefers (Van Parijs, 1997, pp 133-59; White, 1997, pp 323-5).

Critical evaluation of Van Parijs and Mead

Having described the fundamental arguments presented by Mead and Van Parijs, the next step is to evaluate if their frameworks provide an adequate justification of the right to a minimum income. Van Parijs' proposal for an unconditional basic income has been subjected to a number of criticisms. Barry, for instance, argues that a basic income contradicts the spirit of Dworkin's conception of equality of resources that underlies Van Parijs's principle of leximin opportunity. One of the tenets underpinning Dworkin's equality of resources is the principle of special responsibility, which states that, although one must recognise the equal importance of the success of all human lives, individuals have a special and final responsibility for their own success (Dworkin, 2002, pp 5-6). In light of this, they can be compensated for being excluded from the labour market, but not for a decision not to work (Barry, 1992, p 139).

Other authors, such as Van Donselaar or White, dispute Van Parijs' rebuttal of the exploitation challenge. Van Donselaar argues that A exploits B if A is better off than she would have been had B not existed, while B is worse off than she would have been had A never existed. Based on this premise, Van Donselaar argues that a basic income funded from the employment rents would produce an exploitative situation, where individuals who do not want to work take unfair advantage of the redistribution of job resources they were not interested in anyway (see White, 2000, pp 529-30; Widerquist, 2001, pp 753-4).

White starts by recalling that the exploitation challenge implies a discussion about the principle of reciprocity. He points out that job assets, in contrast to natural resources or internal endowments, result from a process of social cooperation, whose redistribution must respect the principle of reciprocity. This requires that all individuals who want to share in the benefits of social cooperation have an obligation to make some kind of productive contribution (White, 1997, pp 320-1). According to White, Van Parijs' weak effort principle, although it avoids the production of brute luck inequalities, does not establish a strong enough connection between contribution and retribution, and therefore does not eliminate the possibility of exploitation (White, 1997, pp 324-5).

Bearing in mind the criticisms made by Barry, Van Donselaar and White, it can be argued that an unconditional basic income would unfairly favour those who do not want to work. This seems to give some support to Mead's claim that the provision of a minimum income guarantee should be made conditional to a work requirement. However, this is not to say that one can accept the totality of Mead's argument. In particular, there is significant criticism of Mead's stance on the relation between obligations and opportunities.

Mead's criticism of the competence assumption (Mead, 1997, p 13) reveals some of his own assumptions on the relation between obligation and opportunity. His criticism can be interpreted in two ways. One is that he assumes that there are enough job opportunities available for all unemployed recipients (see Deacon, 2002, p 54). Obligations would be legitimate because everybody had the opportunity to exercise them. However, nowhere in his argument does he explicitly argue that there are enough jobs for everybody. Furthermore, there is no suggestion that public authorities should create work opportunities for individuals to exercise their obligation to work.

Another possible interpretation, which seems more in line with Mead's thought, is that the enforcement of obligations is legitimate regardless of the opportunities available to individuals. This is reflected in his argument that it is the effectiveness of welfare workers in enforcing the recipients' obligations, rather than the availability of jobs in local labour markets, which explains the effectiveness of WIN programmes[10] (Mead, 1986, p 159). However, as even Etzioni recognises (see, 1997, pp 82-3), the enforcement of obligations can only be fair in the context where individuals have an effective opportunity to fulfil their responsibilities.

Besides the issue of opportunities to fulfil one's obligations, Mead has been criticised for failing to recognise the different ways in which individuals can contribute to society. As mentioned earlier, he argues that the duty to work is the most relevant common obligation (1986, p 243). However, some authors, such as Jane Lewis, argue that this focus on paid work undermines the value of unpaid care work, which is performed mostly by women (1998, p 4). This argument can be extended to unpaid work for the community. Mead's focus on paid work disregards the fact that there are non-marketed activities that can contribute to general well-being. André Gorz, for instance, argues that work can only be seen as a source of economic citizenship when it is performed for the benefit of others as citizens. Working in the public sphere is not necessarily to perform some kind of service to an employer, but to fulfil social needs that might, or might not be, expressed through market mechanisms (Gorz, 1992, pp 180-1).

So, it could be concluded that neither Mead nor Van Parijs provide an adequate justification of the right to a minimum income. Contrary to Van Parijs' argument, the right to a minimum income should be made conditional on some kind of contribution requirement, as this would avoid the possibility of unfairly favouring those who do not want to work. Furthermore, contrary to what Mead argues, in order to avoid situations of unbalanced reciprocity, the enforcement of individual obligations must occur in a context where individuals have an effective opportunity to engage in some kind of contributory activity. Furthermore, this requirement should recognise the variety of activities that make a contribution to society.

Beyond Mead and Van Parijs: foundations for an adequate justification of the right to a minimum income

Mead and Van Parijs fail to provide an adequate justification of the right to a minimum income. To some degree this can be explained by the problems intrinsic to their assumptions about the relationship between the individual, the market and society. Van Parijs' argument for an unconditional basic income is aimed at furthering individuals' ability to develop themselves. However, as can be seen from his handling of work-related assets (1997, pp 106-9; White, 1997, pp 320-1), Van Parijs departs from an individualist approach that detaches individuals from their social, cultural and historical background. This explains why Van Parijs disregards the social nature of some of the resources that individuals use to pursue their ends and the obligations that this imposes on them.

Mead's failure to argue for a fair work requirement, on the other hand, stems from two basic assumptions that underlie his communitarian argument: that the interest of society overrides that of individuals; and that the market is the main mechanism that regulates the functioning of society. In this context, the right to a minimum income is seen, not as a form of furthering individuals' ability to develop themselves, but as a subsidiary form of protection that should be designed in a way not to disturb the functioning of society, and the role of the market, as the primary mechanism of social regulation.

This explains Mead's disregard for the need to create additional jobs when these are not available in the labour market. As they do not respond to the needs identified by the market, they therefore make no contribution to society. This also explains Mead's failure to acknowledge the contributory potential of other activities besides paid employment. Although he recognises that the functioning of society depends on other institutions, such as family or religion (Mead 1986, p 246), only market-based employment is seen as making a contribution to society.

Besides explaining the origins of the problems in the arguments posed by Mead and Van Parijs, the previous paragraphs also suggest that a more satisfactory justification of the right to a minimum income is possible. In order to provide an adequate justification, this alternative argument must be set in the context of an ontological framework that gives a normative priority to the development of individuals, but that also recognises that individuals act in a particular social context that provides them with the resources to develop themselves, and requires from them the fulfilment of individual obligations. This would open up the way for the recognition of individual obligations, but at the same time guarantee that any contribution requirement is enforced in a context where individuals have the opportunity to fulfil their obligations. Furthermore, in order to ensure that the contribution requirement recognises the variety of activities that make a contribution to society, this alternative justification should be based on an ontological framework that encompasses a more critical view of the regulatory role of the market, acknowledging the importance of other social institutions, such as the family or the state in the regulation of social life.

Conclusion

This chapter has demonstrated that Mead and Van Parijs, who typify the fundamental standpoints in the literature, fail to provide an adequate justification of the right to a minimum income. Reflecting on the difficulties faced by the authors, it has been argued that an alternative argument is possible. This argument should be set in the context of an ontological framework that puts a focus on the promotion of individuals' personal development, but recognises its social basis and the obligations that it imposes on them, and encompasses a more critical view of the role of the market as a mechanism of social regulation.

Notes

[1] According to Rawls (2001, p 90), these can include rights, liberties, opportunities, income, wealth and the bases of self-respect.

[2] This is confirmed by Van Parijs' attempt to justify his proposal for a basic income in terms of its coherence with Rawls's theory of justice (see Van Parijs, 1997, p 95).

[3] There are two fundamental dimensions to this concept of reciprocity. The first is that of mutual respect, which requires individuals to appeal to reasons that could be shared by other individuals or, if the resolution of conflicts is impossible, to maintain mutual respect. The second is that of mutual dependence (Muhlberger, 2000, p 8).

[4] As, for instance, the ability to be well nourished and sheltered, the ability to avoid escapable morbidity or premature mortality (Sen, 1993, p 31).

[5] Public goods are those kinds of goods that are available for the (indiscriminate) use of all individuals and in which individual consumption does not diminish their availability to other individuals. Merit goods are those that respond to claims of distributive justice or to other moral reasons (White, 2003, pp 101-6).

[6] Some authors, such as Rawls, argue that opportunities should be 'maximised', that is, they should be distributed in such a way that the least advantaged end up with at least the same level of opportunities as the least advantaged under any alternative arrangement. Van Parijs argues that in a free society, the least advantaged person should have opportunities that are no smaller than those that enjoyed by the least advantaged person in other feasible arrangements. Not only that, the 'leximin' criteria demands that if there is another feasible arrangement that is just as good for the least advantaged person, then the next person up the scale must have opportunities no smaller than the second person up the scale in this (current) arrangement (Van Parijs, 1997, pp 25, 95).

[7] Van Parijs accepts that part of the basic income could be provided in-kind, namely as structures that secure the enforcement of self-ownership rights (as for instance, the political and the judiciary system), and goods that one would expect that individuals would normally be interested in buying (such as, clean air, the cleaning of roads, the maintenance of public spaces) or that can have positive externalities on the opportunities of individuals (such as education or public infrastructures) (see Van Parijs, 1997, pp 41-5).

[8] In fact, Van Parijs also examines Rohmer's conception of 'capitalist exploitation' (see 1997, pp 169-78). However, as this refers to asset distribution rather than

the relationship between work and personal return, it will not be included in this analysis.

[9] The difference between the Lutheran exploitation and the strong effort (and consequently the 'weak effort') principles lies in the metrics used to compare individuals' contributions and benefits. The first uses the notional of labour value, which corresponds to the '… amount of unskilled labour that enters on average, given the existing equipment and technology, whether directly or indirectly, in the production of a unit of a given product' (Van Parijs, 1997, p 154). However, according to Van Parijs (1997, pp 153-60), this measure poses some significant problems. As an alternative, Van Parijs suggests that a person's contribution should be measured in terms of the work effort (that is, hours of work), while its benefits should be simply measured in terms of received income. In this sense, the strong effort principle is no more than the Lutheran principle applied through a more precise metric.

[10] Mead does consider the possibility that the behaviour of welfare officers concerning the enforcement of work obligations could be a reaction to labour market conditions (1986, p 161). However, based on the results of interviews with welfare officers alone, he quickly dismisses this hypothesis.

THREE

Justifying a minimum income guarantee: the right to personal development

Reflecting on Mead and Van Parijs' failure to provide an adequate justification of the right to a minimum income, Chapter Two argued that a more satisfactory alternative is possible. This chapter aims to develop a normative framework to provide such justification. As demonstrated earlier, the reason behind Mead and Van Parijs' failure lies in their assumptions about the relation between the individual, the market and society that underlie their work. Therefore, the first step in this endeavour will be to delve into the literature that sets the foundations of modern social and political theory to find an ontological framework from which a more adequate justification of the right to a minimum income can be derived.

Rather than going through a comprehensive review of all the relevant views in classical social and political theory, it seems more useful to focus instead on a restricted number of authors – in this case Emile Durkheim, Karl Marx and John Stuart Mill – who proposed influential views about how society and market condition individuals' capacity to explore their inner abilities. In order to facilitate the comparison between the three authors, we need to look at the conception of human nature that underlies their work. As it identifies the biological and psychological traits of individuals, and the external factors that condition the ability of individuals to realise their true nature (Duncan, 1983, pp 6-7), the notion of human nature provides an interesting analytical tool that facilitates comparison between the authors' views of the relationship between the individual, the market and society.[1] Hence, the following sections look at the conception of human nature that underpins the work of Durkheim, Marx and Mill.

Durkheim, Marx and Mill's conceptions of human nature

Although he refuses to specify the general characteristics of human nature (see Gray, 1996, pp 205-6), we can identify the three main traits of Mill's conception of human nature in his writings on happiness and individuality. The first concerns an individual's tendency for self-realisation. This is evident in Mill's writings on happiness, which he upholds as the ultimate aim in the organisation of social life. In his book *Utilitarianism* (1861), Mill puts forward a pluralistic conception of happiness. Here individual happiness is related to one's own particular needs, endowments and personality. Hence, the search for happiness involves a process of discovery and development of one's endowments (Gray, 1996, p 192; 1998, p xv; Ten, 1996, p 214).

The second trait is a person's capacity for autonomous thought. This is evident in Mill's distinction between higher and lower pleasures. Happiness is not about lower pleasures, but about the activities that allow individuals to make use of their capacity for autonomous thought – the higher pleasures[2] (Gray, 1996, p 192). The third trait is the capacity for deliberate choice. This is evident in Mill's defence of the 'principle of liberty', which states that '... no one's liberty may be constrained save to prevent harm to others' (Gray, 1998, p xv). Mill's aim is not to protect individuals from interference by others, but to secure the conditions for them to attain their individuality, that is, that they adopt a form of life that enables them to realise their particular nature in autonomously chosen activities (Gray, 1998, p xv).

Marx's 'historical materialism' can then be seen as an account of the way in which different socioeconomic systems realise or subvert the fundamental traits of human nature. Marx's conception of human nature is especially visible in his analysis of the alienated character of labour in the capitalist mode of production. The capitalist mode of production is structured in such a way that workers are obliged to sell their labour power to guarantee their physical survival – 'market alienation' (Giddens, 1971, p 228). This alienates individuals from their essence, that is, the free exercise of their creative capacities (Giddens, 1971, pp 228-9; Avineri, 1968, p 72). This is further curtailed by increased specialisation, the impossibility to plan and control the productive process and the repetitive and arid character of industrial production under capitalism – 'technological alienation' (Giddens, 1971, pp 228-9).

From this capacity for conscious creative activity, we can derive the second dimension of Marx's conception of human nature: the social nature of individuals. In opposition to Kantian individualism, Marx sees all human activity as social and other-oriented, that is, it depends on, or affects, other individuals. This explains Marx's criticism of the capitalist mode of production which, as it is founded on the right to private property, cannot be not compatible with the other-oriented character of human production (Avineri, 1968, pp 86-91).

The elimination of private property in the socialist mode of production, as it would abolish the separation between labour and product and offset the conditions that determine the organisation of productive processes, would create the necessary conditions for individuals to develop their conscious creative ability and to recognise their interdependency (Avineri, 1968, pp 88-9). Communist society therefore constitutes the culmination of the historical process of human evolution – the moment where social conditions are the expression of human essence (Forbes, 1983, pp 25-6).

In his theory of social justice, which he develops in his study of *The division of labour in society* (1984),[3] Durkheim puts forward a view of human nature marked by the struggle between two contradictory forces: our individual conscience (or personality), that is, that which each one of us owns and that which differentiates us from others; and our common consciousness, which can be defined as '... a set of beliefs and sentiments common to the average members of a single society which forms a determinate system that has its own life' (Durkheim, 1984, p 84).

The transition from mechanical to organic societies implies the transformation of the articulation between individual personality and collective consciousness in the production of social solidarity (Jones, 1986, p 33; Lukes, 1973, pp 139, 149). While in mechanical societies social solidarity is based on the effacement of individual personalities with regard to collective consciousness, in organic societies it depends on the ability of individual personalities to flourish. This requires both the reduction in the scope of the collective consciousness and a structural change in its content. Whereas in (small-scale) mechanical societies social solidarity depends on a set of very specific and enforceable collective values, in (large-scale) organic societies the common consciousness becomes more abstract, in order to cover the diversity of individuals and experiences. At the same time, the content of the common consciousness changes from a focus on the superior interests of society to a focus on the individual – the 'cult of the individual' (Lukes, 1973, pp 147–58).

In this context, social justice becomes a fundamental condition for the guarantee of social solidarity in organic societies. According to Durkheim, '… the division of labour only produces solidarity if it is spontaneous […] But spontaneity must mean not the absence of any deliberate, formal type of violence, but of anything that may hamper, even indirectly, the free unfolding of the social force each individual contains within himself' (Durkheim, 1984, p 313). In order to be spontaneous, the division of labour must occur in a context of 'absolute equality in the external conditions of struggle' (1984, p 313). This requires the elimination of the direct and indirect constraints to individuals' choices over the best way to exploit their talents.

The elimination of direct constraints on personal development involves the abolition of all the situations where the allocation of social functions is made by criteria other than the merit of individuals. This means the abolition of all forms of institutionalised favouritism – or, in Rawlsian terms, careers open to all (Rawls, 2001, p 68). Furthermore, the elimination of direct constraints also involves the reduction of economic inequalities through the elimination of hereditary transmission of wealth, and support to individuals in disadvantaged positions (Durkheim, 1984, p 315). The elimination of indirect constraints is related to the promotion of contractual justice. A fair exchange, Durkheim argues, implies that goods or services exchanged represent an equivalent social value.[4] For this to happen, the parties need to be under equal conditions in the exchange of goods and services (Durkheim, 1984, p 319).

The social basis of personal development

Having highlighted the differences in the way the three authors conceive the relationship between the individual, the market and society, it is still necessary to determine whose work will provide the better ontological framework from which a more adequate justification of the right to a minimum income can be derived. This will become more evident when we look in more detail at the authors' view of the social character of personal development, and the obligations this might impose on individuals, and the role of the market in the regulation of society.

Mill is ambiguous with regards to the social character of personal development. On the one hand, personal development depends on practical experience. Hence, it can only occur in the context of society. However, personal development also requires a person to reflect on her position, and to detach herself from society – hence the importance of the principle of liberty (Lindley, 1986, p 52; Gray, 1996, p 201). The latter element, though, seems to have more weight in Mill's argument, which explains his disregard for the obligations that the social character of personal development imposes on us. As Gray points out (1996, p 193), the principle of liberty is expected to protect our ability to pursue our happiness, not to demand it.

In contrast with Mill, Marx views society as a fundamental condition for the personal development of individuals. As seen above, Marx sees all human activity as social and other-oriented, that is, it depends on, or affects, other individuals (Avineri, 1968, pp 86-91). However, Marx does not acknowledge that the social character of personal development implies any obligations on individuals. In fact, no obligation would be necessary, as the abolition of private property in communist society would create the necessary conditions for individuals to recognise their interdependency (Avineri, 1968, pp 90-1).

From Durkheim's point of view, personal development can only occur in the context of society. However, in contrast with Marx, the social nature of personal development does imply an obligation to exploit one's talents. This obligation is inscribed in the morality of advanced societies which '… requires us only to be charitable and just towards our fellow-men, to fulfil our task well, to work towards a state where everyone is called to fulfil the function he performs the best and will receive a just reward for his efforts' (Durkheim, 1984, p 338). If necessary, this obligation can be enforced through the use of restitutive sanctions. Unlike repressive sanctions, which are aimed at punishing individuals for a particular crime, restitutive sanctions are intended to restore the normal relationship between the social parts. This can be done either by restoring the exchange between the two parts, or by annulling the exchange altogether (Durkheim, 1984, p 29).

The above seems to attest to the superiority, as far as the issue of the social nature of personal development is concerned, of the ontological framework underlying Durkheim's theory of social justice. In contrast with Mill's utilitarianism, Durkheim's theory of social justice is able to conciliate the normative priority to the development of individuals, recognising that the latter depends on their social context. Moreover, in contrast with Marx, Durkheim acknowledges that the social character of personal development imposes obligations on individuals.

As the following shows, the same seems to apply in what concerns Durkheim's view of the role of the market in the regulation of society. Marx's critical view of the role of the market in the regulation of society is quite evident in his analysis of the alienated character of labour in the capitalist mode of production. As seen earlier, a society that is regulated by private property law – and, therefore, the market – subverts the free and other-oriented character of human activity and of social relations in general (Avineri, 1968, pp 90-1).

Mill's praise of the role of the market in the regulation of society is evident in his defence of laissez-faire. As Schwartz demonstrates (1968, pp 119-23), underlying Mill's defence of laissez-faire is a belief on the efficiency of the market, as opposed to state inefficiency, in satisfying the needs and wants of individuals and of solving conflicts of interests between them. This superiority derives from the system of incentives guaranteed by the existence of property rights, and from the advantages of the price system as an information-gathering mechanism, especially when compared with centralised forms of information gathering. State intervention should be limited to those areas where independent individuals cannot adequately manage by themselves (for example, the guarantee of equal treatment or the provision of education) or where the market fails to provide an adequate regulation (namely, the provision of poverty relief) (Hollander, 1985, p 670).

In the same way as Mill, in his theory of social justice, Durkheim enshrines the market as a fundamental mechanism of social regulation. This is evident in Durkheim's defence of property and inheritance law, as a means of marking the boundaries between the different parts of society (Durkheim, 1984, pp 72-5). This is also evident in the fact that his theory of social justice is mostly concerned with market-based employment. However, this is in contradiction with the spirit of *The division of labour in society*, where he presents a more comprehensive analysis of the mechanisms that regulate social life. For instance, in contrast with Mill, the role of the state here is not solely to supplement the market. It acts as an organ of 'social thought', which interprets the common good and, as it secures respect for individual rights, as an organ of social justice (Giddens, 1986, pp 28, 48-9). Furthermore, acknowledging the organic character of modern societies, Durkheim also stresses the regulatory function of other social institutions, such as the family or professional groups (Durkheim, 1984, pp 17-21, 242-5).[5]

As can be seen, when interpreted in the context of his conception of the functioning of organic societies, Durkheim's theory of justice provides a more attractive framework to analyse the role of the market in the regulation of society than that presented by Mill and Marx. In contrast with Marx, Durkheim recognises the role of the market in identifying and satisfying needs in society. In contrast with Mill, Durkheim acknowledges that the functioning of society cannot depend on the regulatory action of the market alone, but of a variety of social institutions.

So, one can conclude that Durkheim's theory of social justice provides the basis from which a more satisfactory justification of the right to a minimum income can be developed, because it (1) provides an ontological framework that focuses on the promotion of individuals' personal development, but (2) recognises its social basis, and the obligations it imposes; and (3) acknowledges that the functioning of society depends not only on the regulatory action of the market, but also of other social institutions.

From Durkheim's theory of social justice to the right to personal development

Having demonstrated the advantages of the ontological framework underlying Durkheim's theory of social justice, the challenge now is to develop a normative framework that, building on Durkheim's theory of social justice, is able to provide a more adequate justification for the right to a minimum income. As a starting point, and in line with Durkheim's theory of social justice, it can be argued that social solidarity in organic societies depends on the ability of individuals to exploit their talents. This can be guaranteed by instituting a 'right to personal development'.[6] However, in order to be successful, this normative framework must also acknowledge some of the problems that are evident in Durkheim's theory of social justice.

From talents to equal opportunity for personal development according to Durkheim

One of the most evident problems in Durkheim's theory of social justice concerns his narrow understanding of the range of activities that can be considered as fulfilling a social function, and consequently as a space for personal development. As mentioned earlier, Durkheim's theory of social justice seems to be restricted to paid employment, thus neglecting the contributory nature of a diversity of non-paid activities such as care work, community work and so forth (Levitas, 1996, p 12).

To a certain point this reflects a deeper problem which concerns the shortcomings in Durkheim's conception of talents and of how individuals exploit them. Durkheim's position on this can be summarised in five ideas. First, talents are 'hereditary tendencies' (1984, p 310), in the sense that they are related to the internal endowments of individuals. Second, individuals have a limited set of abilities, which limits their potential for personal development (1984, pp 310-11). In Durkheim's own words, '... we are certainly not predestined from birth to any particular form of employment, but we nevertheless possess tastes and aptitudes that limit our choice' (1984, pp 310-11). Third, talents are related to the performance of social functions. Fourth, although the process is open to trial and error, under a context of equality of opportunities, individuals will normally perform the social function they are naturally inclined to fulfil (1984, pp 310, 312). Fifth, despite asserting that talents are related to the performance of social functions, Durkheim tends to relate them solely with paid employment (1984, p 310).

There are evident problems to this. First, Durkheim fails to clarify how individuals discover their talents. For instance, even if one accepts Durkheim's claim that individuals have a limited set of abilities, and that the discovery and use of individual talents is open to trial and error, he fails to acknowledge that this is conditioned by the opportunities available for individuals to put their talents to use. Furthermore, Durkheim also fails to recognise the role of education in the ability of individuals to uncover and develop their talents.

Second, as it departs from an idealised vision of the functioning of society, Durkheim fails to provide a more comprehensive analysis of the processes that regulate the allocation of individuals to social functions. Durkheim presumes that once external conditions of struggle are equalised, social functions are fulfilled by those who are best suited to perform them, thus producing social solidarity (see Durkheim, 1984, pp 311-12, 315). Underlying this view of the production of social solidarity in modern societies is the assumption that the distribution of natural talents matches the distribution of social functions. Only under this condition could all the social functions that guarantee the functioning of society be occupied by those best equipped to perform them, and at the same time avoid the feelings of resentment from the inability of individuals to exploit their talents. However, this assumption is clearly contradicted by empirical reality. The existence of unemployment alone – be it due to market imperfections (such as imperfect information and limits to mobility of labour), or to the effects of technological progress on the demand of certain skills, or the effects of economic cycles – is a clear example of a mismatch between the supply and demand of talents in the labour market (see Hudson, 1988, pp 11-27).

This seriously questions Durkheim's conception of equality of opportunity. It is hard to believe that the removal of institutionalised favouritisms or the elimination of all inherited wealth alone will be enough to guarantee that individuals have the same opportunities to exploit their talents. This confirms Watts Miller's view that Durkheim's theory of justice is more about equality of conditions than equality of opportunity (1996, p 129). So, it can be argued that in order to provide a satisfactory justification of the right to a minimum income, the right to personal development must reflect a more comprehensive understanding of individual talents, how individuals exploit them and of the type of activities that can be considered as fulfilling a social function. The next two sections provide further discussion on these issues.

Individual talents and personal development

In line with Durkeim, it could be argued that talents have a biological/physical basis. However, we should differentiate between a 'basic talent', which refers to a particular physical or sensory endowment, and a 'complex talent', which refers to a combination of a variety of physical or sensory gifts in performing a particular activity (Smith, 2001, p 19). As they are related with the fulfilment of social functions, talents here are conceived in the latter sense.

It should also be pointed out that, although they are solely related to the performance of a social function, individual talents are obviously dependent on the features that secure human agency. Hence, in line with the argument put forward by Doyal and Gough (1991, pp 56-69), the ability of individuals to exploit their talents depends on their cognitive capacity (human intelligence, learning skills, reflective skills), emotional stability and physical condition (physical strength, agility, overall bio-functional equilibrium and so forth).

In line with Durkheim, it should also be recognised that the ability of individuals to exploit their talents is socially conditioned. First, because a person's ability to exploit his/her talents depends on opportunities to exercise them. As Roberts shows (1990, p 1), talents can only be recognised through practical performance. This is to say that individuals hold 'recognisable talents' that are identified when performing a given activity or function, and 'hidden talents' that individuals hold but are unaware of. Hence, personal development depends on opportunities to engage one's talents in the performance of a given activity or social function (Roberts, 1990, pp 2-3).

Second, as Smith's notion of 'impairment-talent transferability' (2001, p 30) suggests, talents are themselves socially constructed. According to Smith, rather than a purely medical and static condition, physical impairments are a social construct, which must be analysed in terms of individuals' participation opportunities. When physical impairments are conceived in these terms, the latter could be reconstructed as talents – the case of the relation between giantism and basketball, is a clear example of this. This opens, of course, new opportunities for individuals to exploit their talents (Roberts, 1990, pp 2-3).

In contrast with Durkheim, we should also recognise that the ability of individuals to exploit their talents is conditioned by education and training. The role of education can be traced back to the importance of cognitive ability for human agency. As Doyal and Gough state, the educational system helps individuals to develop cognitive skills such as use of language, reading or mathematical literacy, which are central for the development of human autonomy (1991, pp 181-4, 214-16). Training, on the other hand, allows individuals to transform their natural talents into skills that can be used in the production of goods or services. The role of training and education becomes even more important in the context of the 'knowledge-based economy', as this requires that education and training systems provide a framework to enable individuals to be engaged in learning throughout their lives – that is, lifelong learning (ILO, 2002, p 12).

Finally, as the existence of unemployment exemplifies, the distribution of opportunities for personal development does not necessarily match the distribution of talents in society. In all cases the state, by improving support to individual job-search, by promoting mobility in the labour market, by promoting the creation of training opportunities, or by promoting policies that increase the consumption of goods and services (Hudson, 1988, p 12), could have a relevant role in increasing opportunities for individuals to exploit their talents.

In comparison to that put forward by Durkheim, the conception of talents and personal development proposed here bears three main advantages. First, it provides a more precise image of the process by which individuals discover their talents. In particular, this new approach demonstrates that the discovery and use of personal talents depends in great part on the availability of opportunities to put individual talents to use.

Second, it acknowledges the role of education in improving the ability of individuals to exploit their talents. This prompts a new understanding of personal development that is not restricted to the use of one's talents in the performance of a given social function, but also involves the improvement of one's human capital. Finally, this new conception provides a more comprehensive analysis of the mechanisms that regulate the allocation of individuals to social functions. This lays the foundation for a more comprehensive conception of equality of opportunities for personal development that requires not only the removal of institutional favouritism or elimination of inherited wealth, but also the existence of effective opportunities for individuals to exploit their talents, be they opportunities to exploit new talents, opportunities that enable impairment–talent transferability, or to participate in education or training.

Social functions and personal development

As mentioned earlier, despite the broadness of Durkheim's notion of social function, his theory of social justice fails to acknowledge the contributory nature of other activities besides paid employment. The purpose here, based on Durkheim's original notion of social function, is to determine what activities respond to social needs. In order to guarantee the success of this endeavour, we can build on Stuart White's notion of civic labour, which emerges in the context of his argument that those individuals who, in the context of just economic institutions, require a high share of the social product available, should be expected to make a contribution to society – which can be done by performing a minimum amount of civic labour (2003, p 77).

In line with Durkheim's notion of social function, civic labour refers to all '… labour that provides a significant service for, or on behalf of, the wider community' (White, 2003, p 97). In order to determine what the activities are that might be considered as a form of contribution to society, we need to identify '… what kind of work is sufficiently valuable to other citizens to count in reciprocation for the goods and services they have supplied' (White, 2003, p 99). The most obvious mechanism to determine the value citizens assign to a given good or service is the market. In light of this, civic labour refers, in the first instance, to market-generated paid employment, or self-employment (White, 2003, p 99).

Nevertheless, White recognises that civic labour is not restricted to market-generated paid employment. According to White, civic labour can include paid employment related to the production of public goods, that is, goods where consumption by one individual does not reduce the amount of goods available for consumption by others, and that are available for the (indiscriminate) use of all individuals; and merit goods, that is, goods that respond to claims of distributive justice (that can be structured around the notion of need) or to other moral reasons (White, 2003, pp 101–3).

White's conception of civic labour also includes work performed in the household, namely parental care and care of the infirm.[7] Parental care work can be seen as providing both a merit good, in the sense that it provides for the needs of children, and a public good, in the sense that it guarantees the intergenerational continuity of society, even for those who do not whish to have children. The care of the infirm, on the other hand, can be seen as a merit good, in the sense that it secures the needs of individuals who cannot take care of themselves (White, 2003, pp 111-12).

White's conception of civic labour, despite its relevance, is not without its problems. Although it acknowledges the existence of other contributory activities besides market-generated paid employment, it does not ascribe to them the same moral value. This is clear when he argues that work performed in the production of public and merit goods can only be considered as a form of civic labour to the point that the provision of these goods is not excessive with regards to societal needs (White, 2003, pp 101-8).[8] This is also clear, when he argues that the basic work expectation, for a person with parental responsibilities should be reduced, depending on the age of the child, to something like half the basic work expectation (White, 2003, pp 115-16). This reflects White's assumption that the market is the most suitable mechanism for identifying the contributory nature of productive activities, which is evident in the fact that he never questions the contributory character of market-generated paid employment used in the production of goods and services that are aimed at fulfilling luxurious tastes, rather than social needs.

A second problem is related to the fact that White neglects the role of non-state organisations in the provision of merit goods. Underlying the notion of social economy (or not-for-profit, or voluntary sector or third sector) is a set of organisations that provide a number of goods and services aimed at fulfilling the needs of individuals and communities that are not satisfied by either the market or the public sector (see Defourny et al, 2001, pp 3-4, 20-5). Hence, any paid or unpaid work carried out within this type of organisation can be said to make a contribution to society.

Despite the problems mentioned earlier, Stuart White's definition of civic labour does provide a way of reconciling Durkheim's broader understanding of social function with its narrower use in the context of his theory of social justice. In this context a social function can refer to:

- market-based paid employment, in the sense that it satisfies needs that other individuals are interested in paying for;
- public sector paid employment, in the sense that it contributes to the production of public and merit goods which are essential for the functioning of society;
- paid and unpaid work in social economy organisations, in the sense that it contributes to the production of goods and services that satisfy social needs that are not met by the market or the public sector;

- parental care, in the sense that it guarantees basic conditions for social reproduction;
- care of infirm, disabled or older individuals, in the sense that it satisfies the needs of those who cannot provide for themselves.

However, in contrast with White's argument, these activities, as they are equally important in guaranteeing the functioning of society, bear the same contributory value. This is particularly important in the case of non-paid work, be it in the household or in voluntary organisations, which should be seen as making a valuable contribution to society as paid employment.

This new conception of social function has particular implications in the way one conceives how individuals exploit their talents. In addition to market-based paid employment, it opens the way for a broadening of the idea of personal development to the performance of various forms of paid and unpaid work. Not only that, it brings about a broader understanding of the way in which individuals can exercise their obligation to exploit their talents.

The right to personal development and the guarantee of a minimum income

Having stated a comprehensive view of what human talents are and how individuals exploit them, we are now in a position to put forward the fundamental premises of the right to personal development. This starts from the premise that the production of social solidarity in organic societies depends on the ability of individuals to exploit their talents, that is the ability to nurture their talents through education and training and to exercise them in the performance of a social function. This can be guaranteed by instituting a right to personal development.

In order for individuals to exercise their right to personal development, it is necessary to secure certain conditions. First of all, bearing in mind the importance of a person's physical condition, cognitive capacity and emotional stability to a person's ability to exploit his/her talents, it is argued that social actors and institutions must first meet the individual's basic consumption needs, namely access to an adequate level of income, healthcare and housing.

The exercise of the right to personal development also requires that individuals must be free to choose the way they want to exploit their talents. In line with Durkheim's theory of justice, this requires the removal of all the norms that restrict access to the whole range of activities that enable a person's personal development; and the removal of all the mechanisms that might indirectly condition or influence a person's choice over the best way to exploit his/her talents.

However, a person's ability to exploit his/her talents does not depend on direct or indirect constraints alone. As the previous section showed, a person needs effective opportunities to exploit them. In light of this, it can be argued that he or she should be provided with opportunities, be it new opportunities to use recognisable talents, opportunities to discover hidden talents (even including the transformation of impairments into new talents), or opportunities to engage in training or education.

Finally, the right to personal development carries with it a corresponding responsibility, a reciprocity requirement. As mentioned earlier, the existence of a right to personal development is justified by the assumption that collective life is dependent on a cooperation process whereby individuals use their talents in the exercise of a given social function. Hence, every individual has a duty, using his/her talents, to participate in the cooperation process that secures the functioning of collective life, and consequently the possibility for other individuals to develop themselves. Furthermore, in line with Durkheim's original framework, this obligation can be enforced through the use of restitutive sanctions.

In light of this last requirement, the right to personal development can be summarised in the following terms:

> Every individual has a right to exploit his/her talents, which can be exercised while performing a social function in society, such as paid employment, unpaid work in social economy organisations or providing care to dependent family members, or improving his/her human capital through education or training. In order to secure this right, social actors and institutions must:
> - meet the individual's basic consumption needs;
> - eliminate direct and indirect constraints to the individual's choices on the best way to exploit his/her talents;
> - provide the individual with opportunities to exploit his/her talents;
> - enforce, through the use of restitutive sanctions, the individual's obligation to exploit his/her talents as to enable the personal development of others.

Having stated the basic premises of the right to personal development, it is still necessary to demonstrate how this can provide a more adequate justification of the right to a minimum income. As seen earlier, one of the fundamental conditions for the exercise of one's right to personal development is access to an adequate level of income. This can be guaranteed by the introduction of a right to a minimum income. However, in line with this framework, the exercise of this right to a minimum income is conditional on the participation in education or training, or the performance of paid employment in the private or public sector; paid or unpaid work in social economy organisations, parental care or care for dependent family members.

This obligation can be enforced through the use of sanctions of a restituitive nature, that is, sanctions that are aimed not at punishing individuals for their behaviour, but to motivate individuals to fulfil their obligations. Nonetheless, this contribution requirement, can only be enforced in a context where individuals have effective opportunities to use recognisable talents, to discover hidden talents (even including the transformation of impairments into new talents), or to engage in training or education.

As demonstrated above, the right to personal development seems to satisfy all the requirements that would certify an adequate justification of the right to a minimum income. By making the right to a minimum income conditional on the obligation to exploit one's talents, it satisfies the requirement that this does not favour those who do not want to work. Furthermore, as it requires that the obligation to exploit one's talents is enforced in a context where individuals have the effective opportunity to exploit their talents, it satisfies the requirement that the right to a minimum income does not produce situations of unbalanced reciprocity. Finally, as it includes participation in education or training, or the performance of paid or unpaid work in social economy organisations, or parental care, or care for dependent family members as a way of satisfying the obligation to exploit one's talents, it satisfies the requirement that the reciprocity requirement attached to the right to a minimum income should recognise the variety of activities that make a contribution to society.

Conclusion

The introduction of activation requirements in minimum income schemes prompted a debate about the justification of the right to a minimum income. The previous chapter showed that Mead and Van Parijs, who typify the fundamental views in this debate, fail to provide a satisfactory justification. Reflecting on the limitations of the arguments posed by the two authors, it was argued that a more satisfactory alternative is possible. This chapter set out to develop a normative framework that could provide a more satisfactory justification for the right to a minimum income.

Building on Durkheim's theory of social justice, it was argued that individuals have a right to personal development, from which a right to a minimum income can be derived. As shown, as it makes the right to a minimum income conditional on a requirement to exploit one's talents, as it recognises the need for individuals to have effective opportunities to exploit their talents and recognises the contributory potential of a variety of social activities, it can be argued that the right to personal development can provide an adequate justification for the right to a minimum income. In light of this, it can be argued that the right to personal development should be used as the normative standpoint to analyse the balance between fairness and effectiveness in the activation of minimum income recipients.

Notes

[1] The existence of something like a 'human nature' is an issue of strong debate. Noam Chomsky argues that only the existence of human nature can justify the drive for scientific knowledge and the existence of political debate. As an example, he asks what justifies people's struggle against injustice. Michel Foucault, on the other hand, doubts that there is such a thing as human nature. Rather than asking if human nature exists, Foucault argues that social scientists should study the way this is used in political discourse (Fitzpatrick, 2001, p 95). The use of the notion of human nature here is in line with Foucault's approach. Rather than arguing for a particular view of human nature, the purpose here is to use the concept as an analytical tool that can help in identifying a standpoint in political theory from which adequate justification for the right to a minimum income can be derived.

[2] This distinction must to be related with what Mill calls the 'laws of the mind' (Smart, 1983, p 44), that is, the psychological mechanisms that determine how practical experience is assimilated and processed by individuals. The most relevant laws in Millian psychology are the 'laws of association'. According to Mill, '... a desire, an emotion, an idea of the higher order of abstraction, even our judgements and volitions when they have become habitual, are called up by association, according to precisely the same laws as our simple ideas' (Mill [1843], quoted by Smart, 1983, p 44).

[3] A second conception of human nature is sketched in his essay *The dualism of human nature and its social conditions* (1914) and is further extended in his later writings on morality. Whereas in *The division of labour in society* Durkheim puts forward a vision of human nature where the individual's personality and the common consciousness complement each other, this later conception puts the interest of society, as a superior moral entity, ahead of the interests of individuals who must restrain themselves from acting on the basis of their internal egoistic appetites (see Lukes, 1977, p 83).

[4] Durkheim's notion of social value provides a metric to compare with the value of the goods and services exchanged in society (see Durkheim, 1984, p 317). However, as Jones points out (1986, p 54) this metric is far from clear. Rather, it implies a complex function between the total effort needed in the production of the goods or services, the intensity of the needs these might satisfy and the satisfaction it affords.

[5] In fact, as the preface to the second edition of *The division of labour in society* attests, as his career develops, Durkheim devotes increasing attention to the role of secondary groups in the production of social solidarity (Durkheim, 1984, pp xxxi–lvii).

[6] Despite the focus given to the relationship between individual rights and organic solidarity in his *The division of labour in society*, Durkheim (1984) never makes a specific connection between rights and social justice. He does this later, in a (posthumous) article published in the Revue Philosophique where he analyses the role of the state as an organ of social justice (Giddens, 1986, pp 45-50). According to Durkheim, '... the progress of justice is measured by the degree of respect accorded to the rights of the individual' (Durkheim [1958], quoted in Giddens, 1986, p 49).

[7] This excludes other forms of household work as, White argues, they fulfil domestic and personal rather than social functions (2003, pp 111-12).

[8] White suggests using a revised version of Dworkin's hypothetical insurance market to identify the amount and range of public and merit goods that respond to claims of distributive justice. This consists of estimating the preferences of the average member of the community concerning the level and range of merit goods they would buy. This mechanism could be complemented by a set of mechanisms, such as deliberative opinion polls and citizens' juries, that improve the deliberative and participatory nature of public decision-making institutions (White, 2003, pp 103-9). As for merit goods that respond to other moral reasons, White argues that the provision of these goods should reflect the preferences of the majority and minority in proportion to their respective tax contributions (2003, pp 101-3).

FOUR

The activation dilemma: a comparative study

As seen in previous chapters, besides the discussion about the terms in which the right to a minimum income can be justified, the introduction of activation requirements in minimum income schemes has prompted a debate about how schemes should balance the need to help recipients to (re)gain their self-sufficiency through paid work, with the respect of their rights (see Chapter One). Having demonstrated that the right to personal development can provide adequate justification for the right to a minimum income, this normative framework will serve as the standpoint from which to analyse the balance between fairness and effectiveness in the activation of minimum income recipients.

As mentioned in Chapter Two, Mead seems to argue that the employment effectiveness of minimum income schemes is more dependent on their ability to enforce recipients' obligation to work than on the opportunities available to them (1986, pp 156-68). The argument that will be put forward here is quite distinct from this. As seen earlier (Chapter Three), underlying the right to personal development is a preoccupation with balancing individuals' rights and responsibilities, the main assumption being that this combination of positive and negative incentives to recipients will act in such a way as to increase the employment effectiveness of minimum income schemes.

There are reasons to believe that investment in active labour market policy (ALMP) would improve the employment prospects of minimum income recipients. For instance, various studies have suggested that direct job creation schemes can effectively improve the employment prospects of participants[1] (see Breen, 1991; De Koning et al, 1994; Lechner et al, 1996). Also, as Meager and Evans suggest (1997, p 59), despite having significant displacement and substitution effects (see Breen and Halpin, 1989; De Koning, 1993), subsidies to employers do create more employment opportunities for hard-to-employ individuals, typical of minimum income schemes. Finally, the existing evidence suggests that in-work benefits such as tax credits (see Hotz et al, 2005 or McKay, 2003, pp 31-3) or earnings supplements (see Gardiner, 1997; Bloom and Michalopoulos, 2001) seem to be very effective at inducing minimum income recipients to take up jobs. In light of this, it can be hypothesised that schemes that create more opportunities for recipients to find work, namely via investment in ALMPs, will be more effective at returning beneficiaries back to the labour market.

This is not to say that sanctions are irrelevant in helping beneficiaries. For instance, studies carried out by Pavetti et al (1996) or Fraker et al (1997), suggest that the threat of sanctions increases recipients' compliance with work requirements.[2] However, given that none of the schemes under analysis excludes the use of sanctions, the focus here is not on the impact of sanctions on the schemes' employment effectiveness per se, but on the impact of restitutive sanctions compared with more repressive sanctions. Unfortunately, there is no direct evidence on this topic. Nonetheless, one can hypothesise that because restitutive sanctions are more focused on the enforcement of recipients' obligations than on their punishment, social workers will be more prone to use them as a way of enforcing recipients' obligation to take a job, and therefore improve the overall effectiveness of the schemes.

Besides the impact of the improvement of opportunities to exploit one's talents and the use of restitutive sanctions, we also need to consider the possible impact of improving the other dimensions of an individual's right to personal development on the employment effectiveness of the schemes. While some could argue that giving social workers more power of discretion over recipients could be a tool to increase the schemes' employment effectiveness, the argument here is that reducing the level of discretion in the schemes that secure the delivery of minimum income schemes would clarify recipients' rights and, most importantly, their responsibilities, and consequently improve the schemes' employment effectiveness.

In contrast, there is a possibility that improving recipients' freedom to exploit their talents, in the sense that it might reduce their availability to take work, could have a negative impact on the employment effectiveness of minimum income schemes. In fact, a study carried out by Bloom and Michalopoulos (2001, pp 10-16) shows that, after a one-year period, labour market attachment-oriented programmes, that is, schemes whose main objective is to get recipients back to work as soon as possible, are more effective in returning recipients back to the labour market than human capital development-oriented schemes. However, it could be argued that the combined effect of increasing opportunities to exploit an individual's talents and using restitutive sanctions would cancel the possible negative impact of improving recipients' freedom to exploit their talents. Therefore, minimum income schemes could still be more effective even if they improved recipients' freedom to choose the best way to exploit their talents.

Finally, we need to consider the possible impact of improving recipients' basic consumption needs on the employment effectiveness of minimum income schemes. There is little discussion that in some cases, such as the provision of health and housing services that help recipients to deal with some of the issues that inhibit them to take up jobs, improving their basic consumption needs would improve the employment effectiveness of minimum income schemes. This is not, however, the case as to the possible implications of adequately satisfying the recipients' income needs.

As seen earlier, there is a body of literature that argues that high benefit rates can cause unemployment traps (see Holmlund, 1998, pp 4-5; Carone and Salomaki, 2001, pp 22-5). There are, however, some problems with the literature that supports this argument. First, it fails to acknowledge the role of the duration of benefits that, in the same way as reducing the level of benefits, reduce recipients' wage demands and, therefore, also impact on the employment effectiveness of unemployment schemes (see Holmlund, 1997, p 5). Second, the labour leisure choice model from which most of this literature has developed is based on the presumption that individuals are free to choose between taking a job and remaining unemployed (Frey and Stutzer, 2002, p 95). However, as seen earlier, this is no longer the case in minimum income schemes. Therefore there are reasons to believe that, in the context of an obligation to exploit one's talents, which is enforced through the use of restitutive sanctions, it is possible to improve the benefit rates of minimum income schemes without hampering their effectiveness.

With this in mind, the second part of this book will test the hypothesis that, because of the way they combine both positive and negative incentives, minimum income schemes that show more respect for the right to personal development, once labour market conditions are accounted for, are more effective at returning recipients to the labour market. As a starting point, this chapter presents the cases that will be put to the analysis and discusses what the best methodological framework is to test this hypothesis.

Minimum income schemes in Europe

This section presents the cases that will be used in the comparative study of the relationship between the employment effectiveness of minimum income schemes and their respect for the right to personal development. Bearing in mind the definition of minimum income provided earlier (see Chapter One), these schemes should then respect the following criteria:

- the scheme should be means tested;
- among others, the scheme should provide a safety-net for unemployed individuals, that is, jobless people who are able/available for work;
- the scheme should be subsidiary to other forms of protection (except in the case of family benefits);
- the scheme should not apply any previous contribution requirements.

The first requirement for the development of this study is the availability of comparative information to measure both the schemes' respect for the right to personal development, and their employment effectiveness. This study benefits from the timely coincidence of a spurt of comparative evidence on the regulatory framework of European minimum income schemes in the period between 1997 and 1999 (see Eardley et al, 1996a; Guibentif and Bouget, 1997; Lødemel and Trickey, 2001; Heikkila, 2001), and the availability of longitudinal micro-data from the European Community Household Panel (ECHP) for that same period. ECHP is a survey that applied a standardised questionnaire to a representative panel of households and individuals in the EU15 member states, between 1994 and 2001.[3] This provides comparable data on the labour force status and sources of income of respondents that are vital for measuring the employment effectiveness of minimum income schemes in Europe (see Chapter Six). As a consequence, although this will raise issues about the timeliness and generalibility of the results produced, this study will focus on European minimum income schemes in effect in the period between 1997 and 1999.

However, not all minimum income schemes are suitable to be put under analysis. In the first place, it is necessary that the cases under analysis – even if they incorporate a certain level of local discretion – have a certain degree of internal uniformity, both with regard to the way that the right to a minimum income is defined and the way that the activation of minimum income recipients is implemented. Unfortunately, this is not the case in Spain, where access to the right to a minimum income is defined at a regional level (see Heikkilä, 2001, p 17). This is also not the case for Belgium, where there is significant regional variation in the activation of minimum income recipients (OECD, 1998, p 119), and Italy, where the activation of minimum income recipients varies from locality to locality (see Heikkila, 2001, p 17). In light of this, it seems advisable to exclude schemes from these countries from this study.

Furthermore, it is important that the cases under analysis reflect the different institutional approaches adopted in the European context (see the typologies of minimum income schemes in Chapter One). In light of this, despite its specificity, it is important to include a case that illustrates the provision of a minimum income in the UK. Since 1996, the provision of a minimum income guarantee in the UK has been done through Jobseeker's Allowance (JSA), which provides a minimum income benefit to unemployed people, and Income Support, which provides income protection for jobless individuals who are not entitled to JSA, that is, who are not able to/available for work (see Ditch and Roberts, 2000, pp 17-21).

Bearing in mind the objective of this study, the focus here is on JSA. This benefit is composed of a contributions-based component, which consists of a flat-rate payment, payable for 182 days, targeted at all unemployed people who have the necessary national insurance contributions; and an income-based component, which is a differential benefit for those individuals who do not have the necessary national insurance contributions or who have exhausted their entitlement to the contribution-based component of JSA (Ditch and Roberts, 2000, p 20). In light of this, despite the comparability problems this will produce (see Chapter Six), the income-based component of JSA will be used as the representative case for the UK.

Finally, the selection of cases must occur in such a way that it amplifies the heuristic potential of the methodological framework adopted to analyse the relationship between the schemes' respect for the right to personal development and their employment effectiveness. As the following sections will show, this methodology gives a fundamental role to Ragin's Qualitative Comparative Analysis (QCA). In order to take full advantage of the heuristic potential of this technique, it is necessary to increase the number and diversity of cases for analysis so as to allow for maximum causal complexity (see Ragin, 1987, p 105).

With this is in mind, whenever there is a relevant change in the definition of entitlement rights or in the activation framework of a given minimum income scheme, the subsequent policy configuration should be treated as an independent case and included in the analysis. For instance, the changes produced by the introduction of the 1998 Act of Active Social Policy in the activation of Danish minimum income schemes led to the creation of a new case for the subsequent period. The same occurred after the introduction of the 1998 Social Assistance Act in Finland, the approval of the 1998 Social Code in Germany, the passing of the 1998 Jobseekers Employment Act (WIW) in the Netherlands and the introduction of New Deal for Young People and the New Deal for Long-term Unemployed in the UK, in 1998. Again one should emphasise that the purpose here is not to evaluate whether the changes in the legislation had an impact on the employment effectiveness of the schemes but to allow for maximum causal complexity.

The comparative study of the relationship between the employment effectiveness of minimum income schemes and their respect for the right to personal development therefore covers the following cases, as shown in Table 4.1.

The *Bundessozialhilfegesetz* (BSHG) was introduced in 1961 and is composed of two components: the *Hilfe* in *besonderen Lebenslagen*, which provides a bridge benefit for emergency situations, and the *Hilfe zum Lebensunterhalt,* which provides income support to individuals who cannot support themselves (Hanesh and Baltzer, 2000, pp 16-17). The focus here is on the latter component. In order to

Table 4.1: List of cases for empirical analysis

Country	Minimum income scheme	Year	Case
Germany	*Bundessozialhilfegesetz*	1997	De – BSHG97
		1999	De – BSHG99
Denmark	*Social Bistand*	1997	Dk – SB97
		1998	Dk – SB98a
Netherlands	*Algemene Bijstandswet*	1997	NL – ABW97
		1999	NL – ABW99
France	*Revenu Minimum d'Insertion*	1998	Fr – RMI98
Portugal	*Rendimento Mínimo Garantido*	1998	Pt – RMG98
Ireland	Supplementary Welfare Allowance	1998	Irl – SWA98
Finland	*Toimeentulotuki*	1997	Fin – TTK97
		1999	Fin – TTK99
UK	Jobseeker's Allowance	1997	UK – JSA97
		1999	UK – JSA99

be entitled to BSHG, individuals must have exhausted all the means to support themselves, register as unemployed with the federal employment authorities (*Bundesagentur für Arbeit* [BfA]), and accept any work or training opportunities that are offered to them (Heikkila, 2001, p 37).

German minimum income recipients are, in principle, not entitled to participate in employment programmes organised by BfA. However, they can participate in *Hilfe zum Arbeit* [Help Towards Work] programmes, organised by local authorities. These programmes might involve subsidised work in the primary labour market or work in non-profit/public welfare sectors (Hanesh and Baltzer, 2000, p 32; Voges et al, 2001, p 85). Nonetheless, minimum income recipients could participate in federal employment programmes through agreements between local municipalities and local BfA agencies (Evans, 2001, p 17). In this context, one should point out the changes introduced by the 1998 Social Code, which replaced the Employment Promotion Act (AFG). This gave local BfA agencies more discretion in implementing ALMP and offered new opportunities for the activation of minimum income recipients (Wunsch, 2005, p 11).

The *Social bistand* (SB) was introduced in Denmark in 1974 and provides a minimum income benefit for individuals who have experienced an event – such as job loss, sickness or divorce – that affects their ability to support themselves, and are willing to take any available job offers. The activation of SB recipients depends on the articulation between the municipalities and the public employment services (PES). Municipalities are responsible for the activation of all minimum income recipients, no matter what their condition. Those whose condition is related to unemployment alone can be integrated in the PES, where they receive the same treatment as those receiving unemployment insurance benefits. Until 1998, local authorities were not obliged to offer activation opportunities to SB recipients (Eardley et al. 1996b, pp 113-15). This changed when the Danish government passed the 1998 Act of Active Social Policy, which introduced a right and a duty to activation. This obliged local municipalities to provide activation opportunities for SB recipients, and a consequent obligation on recipients to accept any suitable job offer, or to participate in activation programmes offered by the municipality (Rosdahl and Weise, 2001, p 167).

The new *Algemene bijstandswet* (ABW) was introduced in 1996 in the Netherlands. In order to be entitled to ABW, individuals must have exhausted all means to support themselves; be available for work, which could mean active job-search, registration with PES, or participation in training or education; and agree to sign a personal plan, defining the steps that needed to be taken to return to the labour market (De Haan and Verboon, 2000, pp 7-8). The framework for the activation of ABW recipients was significantly reformed with the introduction of the 1998 WIW which merged a number of labour market programmes (see van Oorschot and Engelfriet, 2000, pp 27-8). WIW gives the municipalities the responsibility of providing the necessary means for long-term unemployed people to find a job, be it subsidised employment with a regular employer, subsidised employment with a municipal employment organisation, training or a social activation option (van Oorschot and Engelfriet, 1999, pp 27-8; Spies and van Berkel, 2001, p 116).

The *Revenu Minimum d'Insertion* (RMI) was introduced in 1988 in France, although later reformed in 1992. It provides minimum income protection for individuals aged over 25,[4] who cannot support themselves, and agree to sign an insertion contract, which defines the objectives and stages for their social insertion process. This involves an holistic approach that covers a number of areas such as work, training, housing, health, and so on. In this context, the obligation to work is as important as the obligation to better one's health or housing situation (Enjolras et al, 2001, p 50; Gautrat et al, 2000, p 9).

The social insertion of RMI recipients depends on the articulation of the *Conseil Departmental d'Insertion* [Departmental Insertion Council] at the regional level, and the *Commission Local d'Insertion* [Local Insertion Committee] at the local level. The first includes representatives from central government and other authorities concerned with the provision of welfare, employment and training services. Its role is mainly connected with the planning and monitoring of insertion strategies at the regional level. Local Insertion Committees are responsible for the preparation, monitoring and evaluation of insertion contracts, and for the creation of partnerships that can further the social insertion opportunities of RMI recipients (Enjolras et al, 2001, pp 46-7; Gautrat et al, 2000, pp 14-16; Evans, 2001, pp 14-15).

The *Rendimento Mínimo Garantido* (RMG) was introduced in 1996 in Portugal on an experimental basis and came to full implementation in July 1997. In order to be entitled to minimum income protection, individuals must have exhausted all means to sustain themselves and agree an insertion contract, which defines their rights and responsibilities in the social insertion process. In particular, recipients are required to be available to work or to attend an education/training course; to participate in temporary activities that can further their future employability, or that satisfy social and environmental needs; and to engage in processes, such as having medical treatment, improving housing conditions, and so on, that promote their social insertion (Capucha, 1998, p 38; Cardoso and Ramos, 2000, p 15).

The social insertion of RMG recipients is ascribed to *Comissões Locais de Acompanhamento* [Local Support Committees]. These bodies comprise representatives from central government agencies, local municipalities and local organisations, and are responsible for the definition, implementation and evaluation of insertion contracts. Despite the initial intention of decentralising local delivery, the Ministry of Solidarity and Social Security has a leading role in the delivery of the measure. This is evident in the fact that the ministry provides the majority of material resources that secure the implementation of the measure, and in the fact that the head of the Local Support Committees is nominated by the ministry (Capucha, 1998, pp 32-6; Cardoso and Ramos, 2000, p 16).

The Supplementary Welfare Allowance (SWA) was introduced in 1993 in Ireland, but was revised in 1995. It provides a minimum income benefit to individuals who cannot support themselves, and who are registered with the Training and

Employment Authority (FAS) (Eardley et al, 1996b, pp 215-16; Collins, 2000, p 11). The main responsibility for the activation of SWA recipients lies with FAS, which runs the majority of employment-related activation programmes. Nonetheless, the Department of Education and Science, the Revenue Commissioners and the Department for Social, Community and Family Affairs, which has its own Employment Support Service, also play a role in the activation of SWA recipients (Eardley et al, 1996b, p 214; Collins, 2000, pp 15-16).

The *Toimeentulotuki* (TTK) was introduced by the 1984 Social Welfare Act in Finland, and was revised with the introduction of the 1998 Social Assistance Act. In the same way as its predecessor, the 1998 Social Assistance Act makes no explicit obligation to find work. In fact, an appeal court ruling stated that claimants did not have an automatic obligation to take paid work (Eardley et al, 1996a, pp 128-9; OECD, 1998, p 15). Nonetheless, recipients are expected to register with the PES and to present proof of active job-search. Not only that, they will be subjected to sanctions in case they fail to look for jobs or to take part in activation measures (Heikkila and Keskitalo, 1999, p 9; Heikkila, 2001, p 31). If anything, as it increased benefit sanctions and reduced benefit rates, this Act has increased the focus on the activation of recipients (Heikkila and Keskitalo, 1999, p 9). The activation of TTK recipients is mainly the responsibility of employment authorities. Nonetheless, some local authorities have engaged in the creation of employment projects for minimum income recipients (Heikkila and Keskitalo, 2000, p 31).

The Jobseeker's Allowance (JSA) was introduced in October 1996 in the UK. As mentioned earlier, the scheme involves a contributions and an income-based component. In order to be entitled to JSA, individuals must sign a Jobseeker Agreement, and engage in active job-search. This can include applying for jobs, seeking information from advertisements and companies, registering with private employment agencies, preparing a CV, building a list of possible employers, or looking for information on alternative occupations (Ditch and Roberts, 2000, p 21).

In 1998, the British government introduced the New Deal for Young People (NDYP) and the New Deal for Long-term Unemployed (NDLTU), with the purpose of increasing the opportunities of JSA recipients to find work. The NDYP is compulsory for all individuals aged between 18 and 24 who have been receiving JSA for more than six months and involves three main stages: the 'gateway', the 'New Deal options' and the 'follow through' stage. The gateway phase consists of four months of assisted job-search. In the case of unsuccessful job-search, recipients are obliged to take part in a New Deal option, be it subsidised employment, full-time education and training, work in the voluntary sector, or work in the Environment Task Force. After this period, unemployed recipients are given a six-month follow-through period of assisted job-search. The NDLTU is targeted at JSA recipients who have been unemployed for at least two years. The programme includes advisory interviews, employer subsidies and access to work-based training (Ditch and Roberts, 2000, p 33).

Ragin's qualitative comparative analysis: a step forward in social enquiry

As seen earlier, given the restrictions in the data available for analysis, this comparative study will build on the evidence from 13 cases. However, a number of issues have been raised about the reliability of the results of studies that use only a small number of cases for comparative analysis, as opposed to those that work with large samples. One of the most common criticisms is that this will lead to a situation where the number of cases is not much higher than the number of variables for analysis – the 'many variables, few cases' problem. According to Goldthorpe (1997, p 5), when multivariate analysis techniques are in use, a small sample reduces the degrees of freedom, creates problems in dealing with intercorrelations between independent variables and makes multivariate models 'overdetermined', thus reducing the researchers' ability to produce robust results. Another problem, according to Lieberson (1991, pp 317-18), refers to the fact that these types of studies are (especially) vulnerable to the purposeful distortion of the selection of cases by researchers as a means to ensure that the empirical analysis produces the expected results.

Most importantly, critics would argue, while large quantitative studies (as they rely on statistical tools of analysis) produce propositions of a probabilistic nature, small–N studies (as they rely on logical techniques of analysis)[5] tend to produce deterministic propositions. In simpler terms, whereas quantitative studies try to determine if the presence of variable X can increase the probability for outcome Y to occur, small–N studies try to determine if the presence of X will produce Y (Lieberson, 1991, p 309; Goldthorpe,1997, pp 4-5).

Unfortunately, Lieberson argues (1991, pp 309-12), in order to be adequately validated, deterministic inferences require a number of situations that rarely occur in social inquiry. First, they require that the researcher knows all the factors that influence the outcome under analysis, and has measurable data on all of them. Second, they require that there are no errors in the measurement of both dependent and independent variables that might bias the analysis. Third, they require that the outcome under analysis is not affected by random events. Given the recurrence of this type of situation in social life, Lieberson concludes (1991, p 309), it is more adequate to look at social causation in probabilistic terms.

As can be seen, most of these criticisms rely on the assumption (which derives from their reliance on statistical tools of analysis) of the superiority of variable-oriented comparative studies. However, there are several criticisms to this pretence of superiority. This is the case of Ebbinghaus (2005), which questions the randomness of the samples used in comparative quantitative analysis. Quantitative research depends on the availability of comparable data for analysis. However, there is a bias in the availability of this type of evidence. As Ebbinghaus points out (2005, p 136), quantitative comparable evidence is more likely to be available in countries with more advanced economies, with a larger population, with stable democratic political systems and that are members of international organisations that collect and disseminate comparative data. If the evidence used in quantitative comparative studies is not randomly distributed, Ebbinghaus concludes, then one must question their ability to produce generalisable statements.

While Ebbinghaus focuses on the empirical limitations of quantitative comparative studies, others such as Ragin (1987), concentrate on the underlying methodological limitations of the statistical techniques used in these types of studies. While admitting the comparative advantage of quantitative studies in producing generalisable results, Ragin criticises the additive model of causation that underlies these studies for the fact that they do not acknowledge the multiple conjunctural character of social causation, which is at the centre of case-oriented comparative research (Ragin, 1987, pp 58-61).

Multivariate statistical techniques rely on the assumption that the effect of variable X on outcome Y is the same for all cases, and does not depend on the value of the other independent variables (Ragin, 1987, pp 58-64). By assuming that the effect of a given variable is independent of the value of other independent variables, quantitative studies neglect the conjunctural character of social causation, in the sense that social phenomena are the product of the intersection of various conditions in a given time and space. By assuming that the effect of a given variable is the same for all cases, it neglects the multiple nature of social causation, in the sense that the same outcome can be the product of different combinations of causal conditions (Ragin, 1987, p 27).

In an attempt to propose an alternative technique that, even with a small number of cases, is able to uncover processes of multiple conjunctural causation and produce generalisable results, Ragin puts forward his qualitative comparative analysis (QCA) technique. QCA departs from the premise of maximum causal complexity. Each case is seen as a combination of different causal conditions, which are understood in relation to one another, and constitute a particular configuration. Furthermore, it assumes that a given outcome is the product of one (or more) combination(s) of causal conditions (Ragin, 1987, pp 52, 92-3).

QCA uses Boolean algebra to simplify the complexity in social reality and uncover processes of multiple conjunctural causation. The basic premise of Boolean algebra is that a given outcome is the product of the presence (or absence) of one, or more, causal conditions. Therefore, in QCA both dependent and independent variables are represented through a binary variable, which measures if a given condition is present or absent.

Take the following example. As can be seen in Table 4.2, the outcome Y is the product of a variety of combinations. (For the purpose of presentation, the presence of a given condition is represented in uppercase, while its absence is represented in lower case.) These can be represented in a truth table (see Table 4.3). Here, each logical combination is represented as one row in the truth table using a binary scale where '1' represents the presence of a causal condition and '0' represents its absence. Once this part of the truth table is constructed each row is assigned an output value. Again, '1' represents the presence of the outcome variable and '0' represents its absence. Finally, in order to map the relative importance of each

Table 4.2: List of hypothetical combinations for analysis

Case	
1	ABc = Y
2	ABC = Y
3	Abc = y
4	abc = y
5	AbC = Y
6	ABC = y

Table 4.3: Hypothetical truth table

A	B	C	Y	Number of cases
1	1	0	1	2
1	1	1	1	1
1	0	1	1	1
1	0	0	0	1
0	0	0	0	1

logical combination in the sample under analysis, it is convenient to include the frequency, that is, the number of cases, of each combination (Ragin, 1987, p 87).

Once the various combinations are mapped in the truth table, the researcher can make use of a number of Boolean rules to further reduce the complexity in the sample and to uncover processes of multiple causation – a process otherwise known as Boolean minimisation. The most important of these rules states that 'If two Boolean expressions differ in only one causal condition yet produce the same outcome, then the causal condition that distinguishes the two expressions can be considered irrelevant and can be removed to create a simpler, combined expression' (Ragin, 1987, p 93). This process of Boolean minimisation is conducted in a bottom–up manner in the sense that it seeks to identify simpler combinations of causal conditions and produce parsimonious explanations.

If one takes the hypothetical cases described above, it is possible to say that:

$$Y = ABc + AbC + ABC$$

where '+' means OR

That is to say, that outcome Y is the product of three different combinations: when variables A and B are present, and variable C is absent; or when variables A and C are present, and variable B is absent; or when variables A, B and C are all present. However, if one applies the minimisation rule mentioned earlier, the two latter combinations can be minimised into a simpler expression:

$$Y = ABc + AC$$

This is to say, that Y is the product of the combination of variables A and B, with the absence of C; or the presence of variables A and C, regardless of B being present or absent. One should nonetheless notice the role of variable A in producing outcome Y. As can be seen above, for Y to occur, it is always necessary for variable A to be present. In QCA, causation is described in terms of necessity, that is, when a cause is always present when an outcome occurs; and sufficiency, that is, when a cause can produce the outcome by itself. In this particular case variable A is a necessary but not sufficient causal condition.

Given the complexity of social life, the researcher must search for the different combinations of necessity and sufficiency. For instance, if there is only one cause to the outcome, then it could be said that the causal condition is both sufficient and necessary. If various causes can produce the outcome by themselves, these are sufficient, but not necessary causes. Finally, if a cause only appears in a subset of combinations that produce the outcome, then this causal condition is neither necessary nor sufficient. This latter situation is the one that best expresses the combinatorial nature of Ragin's QCA, in the sense that it suggests social phenomena result from the combination of various causal conditions (Ragin, 1987, pp 99–100).

In addition to the use of Boolean algebra, there are four distinctive features in QCA that merit further mention. The first concerns the way in which it deals with the issue of case selection. In contrast with traditional quantitative studies, QCA is not concerned with the number of cases, but with allowing maximum causal complexity (Ragin, 1987, p 105). Therefore, the main concern of the researcher is to determine to what degree the cases under analysis are able to represent all the possible logical causal combinations that might produce the phenomena under analysis (Ragin, 1987, pp 13-14). This has a major implication for the selection of cases. Rather than adding new cases for the sake of increasing the size of the sample, the main aim of the researcher is to select cases that capture, as much as possible, all the different combinations of variables available for analysis.

The second feature of QCA concerns the way in which cases are conceived and analysed. QCA is both holistic and analytic. Cases are seen as a combination of its parts. In line with holistic canons, this means that a change in a single part of the whole will alter the whole nature of the whole (Ragin, 1987, pp 126-7). This has a particular implications for the analysis of the role of time in explaining social causation. According to Ragin (1987, pp 55–61), the ability of quantitative studies to produce generalisable propositions partly depends on the assumption that, given their structural character, social phenomena tend to change very slowly. This rather diminishes the role of time in the analysis of causal processes. In contrast, QCA tends to emphasise the role of the historical context in explaining social phenomena. This implies, of course, an entirely different conception of causality. Whereas traditional quantitative comparative studies presume that causal relations are permanent, QCA assumes that causality is context (and conjuncture) sensitive (Rihoux, 2006, p 682).

Third, compared with traditional case-oriented studies, QCA provides a clear framework to evaluate to what degree a given empirical proposition can be generalisable to non-observed cases. This can be done by assuming that all non-observed cases will not produce the outcome under analysis and to apply the Boolean minimisation procedures to all possible logical combinations (see Ragin, 1987, pp 108-9). Accepting the severity of such an assumption, one should nonetheless emphasise Ragin's effort to clarify the terms in which QCA can produce generalisable results.

Finally, QCA requires a constant reciprocal relation between theory and evidence. This is especially evident in the way QCA deals with the existence of contradictory cases, that is, situations where similar cases produce different outcomes (Ragin, 1987, p 113). Although QCA possesses Boolean procedures that assist researchers in dealing with this problem (see Ragin, 1987, pp 113-18), Ragin suggests that the best option here is to follow the lead of case-oriented researchers and to try to re-examine the evidence in light of the theoretical framework and to try to refine the measurement of both dependent and independent variables, or to identify any omitted variables in the framework. In case this fails, the other option is to re-engage in data collection so as to increase the number of combinations for analysis (1987, pp 115-16).

In search for a more comprehensive methodological framework

So, it is possible to identify a number of advantages in using QCA in this study. Compared with the traditional variable-oriented approach, QCA is particularly well equipped to produce parsimonious explanations about the relationship between the employment effectiveness of minimum income schemes and their respect for recipients' right to personal development with such a restricted number of cases for analysis (Ragin, 1987, pp 121-2). Secondly, as Ragin shows (1987, pp 118-21), QCA is especially well equipped to test the empirical validity of theoretical arguments. Making use of the properties of Boolean algebra, QCA is able to formalise theoretical arguments and to map areas of agreement and disagreement between a given theoretical model and the empirical results. Not only that, QCA allows the researcher to identify causal combinations that are not hypothesised by the theoretical model of analysis.[6]

But QCA is not without it problems, which have to be considered if QCA is to be used in this study. One of the basic criticisms of Ragin's method is that the use of crisp dichotomies to analyse social reality, besides disregarding the possibility of measurement errors, involves a significant loss of information, which limits its analytical potential (Kangas, 1994, p 361). In addition, QCA has been criticised for its reliance on logical and non-statistical tools of analysis typical of case-oriented studies. As with traditional case-oriented studies, QCA can only function under the assumption that social reality can be classified in terms of clear-cut dichotomies, that there are no random effects, and that all relevant variables have been identified (Goldthorpe, 1997, pp 7-8; Bennett, 1999, pp 18-19).

Another problem concerns the instability of the results produced by QCA. Given its logical nature, a simple alteration in the value of one of the causal conditions can completely change the results of the analysis (see Kangas, 1994, p 361; Bennett, 1999, pp 18-19). This instability is reinforced by the fact that QCA is dependent on the selection of cases, that is, when applied to different cases it might produce different results (Swyngedouw, 2004, p 162). This limits, of course, the ability of QCA to produce general explanatory statements.

Finally, as Janoski and Hicks would argue (1994, p 17), QCA discards too easily the value of additive models of causation. According to Janoski and Hicks, the identification of patterns of association, as in the case of QCA, does not necessarily have more explanatory potential than the identification of patterns of variation. When compared with traditional quantitative methods, QCA limits the researcher's ability to identify the relative importance of explanatory variables. This might lead to an over-exaggeration of the importance of less relevant variables (or configurations), or even spurious causation (Kangas, 1994, p 361; Goldthorpe, 1997, pp 7-8; Nelson, 2004, p 114).

Although one cannot disregard the criticisms made of QCA, some of them might be somewhat exaggerated. For instance, binary sets can be made more flexible in order to incorporate both qualitative and quantitative differences. In fact, the researcher can test how different cross-over points impact in the analysis of causal relations, hence reducing the possibility of loss of information. The same applies to the charge regarding the volatility of the results produced by QCA. The likelihood of measurement errors can be reduced through an effective manipulation and understanding of the cases under analysis and of the foregoing theoretical framework. Finally, it can also be argued that the focus on combinations, rather than on variables, limits the dependency on the selection of cases.

However, if the problems of loss of information and the volatility of the results produced by QCA can be, if not eliminated, considerably reduced, the same cannot be said about the QCA's limitations in measuring the relative importance of explanatory variables, and its vulnerability to spuriousness charges. As a response to this (and other) criticism(s) Ragin proposed an alternative technique: fuzzy-set analysis (2000).[7] Fuzzy-set analysis expands the logic of QCA with the use of fuzzy-sets, which measure the cases' set membership in a scale from 0 to 1, where 1 represents full membership and 0 represents full non-membership (Ragin, 2000, p 160). However, in contrast with QCA, fuzzy-set analysis involves the use of probabilistic tools of analysis. Although it seems better equipped to retain the richness of the data under analysis, fuzzy-set analysis is not able to deal with a small number of cases as successfully as QCA, and therefore does not really constitute a valid alternative for this study (Rihoux, 2006, p 685).

In light of this, it seems advisable to follow the example given by Kangas (1984) and others (see, Rihoux, 2006, p 696), and to try to combine QCA with traditional statistical tools of analysis. As Ragin himself admits (1987, pp x-xi), there are advantages to this. As they are based on an additive model of causation, statistical techniques are able to identify patterns of co-variation that Boolean algebra cannot measure. This, in turn, will capture the relative importance of explanatory variables in explaining a given outcome. Furthermore, as they depart from a probabilistic premise, statistical tools will reduce the impact of measurement errors on the results produced by QCA.

Bearing in mind this study's objective, two quantitative tools can be identified that, in combination with QCA, could be extremely useful in the analysis of the relationship between the employment effectiveness of minimum income schemes and their respect for the right to personal development: correlational tools and cluster analysis. As this study involves a small number of cases, it seems more adequate to use simple correlation measures, namely Pearson's product moment correlation coefficient (r), rather than more sophisticated tools such as multiple regression analysis (see Fielding and Gilbert, 2000, pp 165-8). In contrast with QCA, correlational tools are better equipped to capture patterns of co-variation and to measure the relative importance of the different variables in explaining the employment effectiveness of minimum income schemes.

Although it is not a technique for causal analysis, cluster analysis does provide an interesting alternative for analysing the relationship between the schemes' respect for the right to personal development and their employment effectiveness. Taking advantage of the analytical power of hierarchical and K-means cluster analysis, the purpose here is to use the information on internal consistency of the various clusters and on the relative importance of the various variables in the clustering process to explain the differences in the employment effectiveness of the minimum income schemes under analysis.

Conclusion

Having made the argument as to why the right to personal development can adequately justify the provision of a minimum income guarantee, the second part of this book will test the hypothesis that minimum income schemes that show more respect for the right to personal development, once labour market conditions are accounted for, are more effective at returning recipients to the labour market. After a brief description of the cases under analysis, it has been argued that the relationship between the employment effectiveness of minimum income schemes and their respect for the right to personal development can best be analysed by combining the heuristic potential of QCA, simple correlational tools and cluster analysis.

The following chapters of this book engage in an empirical study to test the hypothesis advanced earlier. Chapter Five starts by measuring the respect for recipients' right to personal development in the minimum income schemes under analysis. Chapter Six then looks at the schemes' employment effectiveness. In line with the methodological framework designed here, Chapter Seven uses QCA, simple correlational tools and cluster analysis to study the relationship between the schemes' employment effectiveness and their respect for recipients' right to personal development. The final chapter looks back at the both the theoretical and empirical ideas that emerge from this book and raises implications for policy makers.

Notes

[1] However, other studies, such as Ackum (1995), Disney et al (1992), Spitznagel (1989) or Bonnal et al (1994) show little or no long-term impact on recipients' employment chances and significant displacement effects.

[2] As seen earlier, the impact of sanctions on the employment effectiveness of minimum income schemes depends not only on the preventive effect of the threat sanctions, but also on the impact of the enforcement of sanctions. For instance, in the UK, New Deal personal advisers suggested that jobseekers that were sanctioned with a 26-week benefit suspension increased their job-search efforts (Saunders et al, 2001, p 41). However, the focus here is solely on the impact of the threat of sanctions.

[3] The first wave, back in 1994, only included 12 member states. Since then, Austria (1995) and Finland (1996) and Sweden (1997) have joined the project. See http://forum.europa.eu.int/irc/dsis/echpanel/info/data/information.html

[4] Except those with children (Gautrat et al, 2000, p 9).

[5] As Ragin points out (1987, pp 36-9), case-oriented studies seem to rely heavily on Mill's methods of agreement and difference as strategies for establishing empirical generalisations. Mill's method of agreement presumes that, if a person wants to know the cause for Y to occur, they should identify instances when Y occurs and determine which variable invariably precedes its occurrence. The method of difference involves two distinct moments. In a first moment, the researcher applies the method agreement to the cases where Y occurs, and then to those where Y does not occur. The method then presumes that, when comparing the result of the two operations, where there are variables that do not differ, those variables that do differ can explain the variation in the outcome variable.

[6] QCA also allows the researcher to model causal combinations that were hypothesised by the theoretical model, but found not to produce the outcome (Ragin, 1987, pp 118-21).

[7] Another attempt to overcome some of these criticisms was multi-value QCA (MV-QCA), put forward by Cronqvist and Berg-Schlosser (2005). MV-QCA can be considered a direct extension of QCA in the sense that allows researchers to use multivalue, rather than simple, dichotomous variables (Rihoux, 2006, p 685). Unfortunately, as it is not as able to deal with a small number of cases as successfully as QCA, MV-QCA does not really constitute a valid alternative for this study (Rihoux, 2006, p 685).

FIVE

Measuring respect for the right to personal development

In line with the plan of analysis outlined earlier, the purpose of this chapter is to measure the respect for recipients' right to personal development in the schemes under analysis. As seen earlier, this normative framework states that every individual has a right to exploit his/her talents, which can be exercised while performing a social function in society, such as paid employment, unpaid work in social economy organisations or providing care to dependent family members, or improving his/her human capital through education or training. In order to secure this right, social actors and institutions must:

- meet the individual's basic consumption needs;
- eliminate direct and indirect constraints to the individual's choices on the best way to exploit his/her talents;
- provide the individual with opportunities to exploit his/her talents;
- enforce, through the use of restitutive sanctions, the individual's obligation to exploit his/her talents as to enable the personal development of others.

The next sections look at the institutional features that best reflect the spirit of this normative framework. In order to best assess how the various schemes compare, the final section then combines these features as an index of respect of the right to personal development

Provision of an adequate level of income

The obvious start for this exercise will be to look at how schemes satisfy recipients' basic consumption needs. As seen earlier, these can include the need for an adequate level of income, healthcare and adequate housing. However, bearing in mind the mediating role of income in accessing healthcare and adequate housing, the focus here is on the level of income recipients receive. Hence, the purpose is to measure to what degree minimum income schemes provide a level of income that allows recipients to fully participate in society.

Assuming that each individual requires a minimum level of income to fully participate in society, which can be identified by what is know as a 'poverty line', this can be measured by comparing recipients' 'total household net disposable income'[1] – or more succinctly, disposable income – with the value of the poverty line (here set at 60% of the median equivalised income[2]) of their country of residence (Eurostat, 2003b, p 3).

As can be seen in Table 5.1, none of the schemes under analysis fully satisfies the requirement that each recipient must be provided with a level of income that allows them to fully participate in society. The ABW in the Netherlands and SB in Denmark are the schemes where the recipients' income needs are better satisfied. The SWA in Ireland should also be noticed, as all households have a disposable income of at least 70% of the value of the poverty line. On the other hand, RMG in Portugal and BSHG in Germany are the schemes where the recipients' disposable income is further away from the poverty line.

It can also be observed that some schemes pay more attention to the needs of particular households. For instance, RMI in France, ABW in the Netherlands and JSA in the UK seem to discriminate in favour of lone-parent families. The SB in Denmark and SWA in Ireland tend to privilege couples (with or without children). The RMG in Portugal, BSHG Germany and TTK in Finland, on the other hand, seem to favour households with children.

Finally, between 1997 and 1999 there was a noticeable decrease in the disposable income of families on TTK in Finland, especially households with children. This appears to be associated with the introduction of the 1998 Social Assistance Act that imposed reductions in benefit rates (Heikkila and Keskitalo, 2000, p 10). In

Table 5.1: Disposable income as a percentage of the poverty line

	Single	Lone parent + 2 children[a]	Couple (no children)[a]	Couple + 2 children[a]	Disposable income as a percentage of the poverty line $(\Sigma/4)^b$
De – BSHG97	0.38	0.62	0.46	0.61	0.52
De – BSHG99	0.38	0.63	0.46	0.62	0.52
Dk – SB97	0.76	0.78	0.92	0.93	0.85
Dk – SB98	0.75	0.97	0.91	0.92	0.89
NL – ABW97	0.99	1.00	0.94	0.94	0.97
NL – ABW99	0.99	1.00	0.94	0.92	0.96
Fr – RMI98	0.54	0.71	0.55	0.62	0.61
Pt – RMG98	0.39	0.56	0.50	0.63	0.52
Irl – SWA98	0.70	0.71	0.75	0.74	0.73
Fin – TTK97	0.54	0.78	0.61	0.78	0.68
Fin – TTK99	0.51	0.70	0.57	0.70	0.62
UK – JSA97	0.51	0.65	0.54	0.61	0.58
UK – JSA99	0.51	0.73	0.54	0.57	0.59
Average					0.68

Notes: [a] Scoring criteria: proportional score, where 1 refers to a situation where value of disposable income is equal to, or higher than, the value of the poverty line.
[b] The values in this column represent the mean value of the previous columns.

contrast, in the same period, there was an increase in the disposable income of lone-parent families on SB (Denmark) and JSA (UK). Nonetheless, in the UK this was accompanied by a decrease in the disposable income of couples with children.

Freedom to choose other activities instead of paid employment

Having looked at how minimum income schemes satisfy the recipients' basic consumption needs, we now turn to the freedom they have to exploit their talents. As seen earlier (see Chapter Three), here we need to look at both the direct and indirect constraints to individuals' choices over the best way to exploit their talents. Reflecting on the literature on activation (see Chapter One), two situations can be identified where recipients face a direct constraint on their ability to choose the best way to exploit their talents.

The first concerns the choice of the types of activities recipients are allowed to perform as a means of fulfilling their activation requirement. Traditionally, minimum income schemes tend to assume that only paid employment and/or participation in education/training are the most adequate ways to fulfil this requirement (Guibentif and Bouget, 1997, pp 15-16). As argued earlier, this does not acknowledge the value to both recipients and society in general of other activities such as care or voluntary work (see Chapter Three). The purpose here, then, is to determine how free recipients are to perform other activities instead of paid employment as a form of activation, be it education/training, performing voluntary work in social economy organisations or providing care to children or dependent adult relatives.

As can be seen in Table 5.2, the RMG in Portugal, BSHG in Germany and ABW in the Netherlands are schemes where minimum income recipients have more freedom to choose other activities instead of paid employment. In contrast, the SWA in Ireland and JSA in the UK are cases where there are more constraints on recipients' choices. Nonetheless, in the UK, the introduction of New Deal programmes in 1998, which brought in education and training options for those on JSA, prompted a significant increase in the recipients' freedom of choice (Ditch and Roberts, 2000, pp 32-3).

The low score of the French RMI reflects the paternalistic character of the social exclusion paradigm that underlies it (Jordan, 1996, pp 3-4). As it focuses on the negotiation between the social worker and the recipient during the social insertion process, recipients' freedom to choose the types of activities they wish to perform is less regulated. This explains why this scheme scores so low in this respect. However, as it also privileges an holistic conception of social insertion, which puts the obligation to work at the same level with other obligations such as attending education or securing adequate housing, one must acknowledge that the criterion adopted here might underestimate RMI (and RMG) recipients' freedom to choose the types of activities they wish to perform.

Table 5.2: Freedom to choose other activities instead of paid employment

	Freedom to participate in education[a]	Freedom to participate in training[a]	Freedom to provide childcare[a]	Freedom to provide other family care[a]	Freedom to perform unpaid work in social economy organisations[a]	Freedom to choose other activities instead of paid employment ($\sum$/5)[b]
De – BSHG97	0.5[1]	0.5[1]	1	1	0	0.60
De – BSHG99	0.5	0.5	1	1	0	0.60
Dk – SB97	1	1	0.5[3]	0	0	0.50
Dk – SB98	1	1	0.5[3,4]	0	0	0.50
NL – ABW97	1	1	1[5]	0	0	0.60
NL – ABW99	1	1	1[5]	0	0	0.60
Fr – RMI98	0.5[2]	1	0	0	0	0.30
Pt – RMG98	1	1	0.5[3]	0.5[3]	0	0.60
Irl – SWA98	0.5[2]	1	0	0	0	0.30
Fin – TTK97	1	1	0.5[3]	0	0	0.50
Fin – TTK99	1	1	0.5[3]	0	0	0.50
UK – JSA97	0	0	0.3[6]	0.3[6]	0	0.12
UK – JSA99	0.5[2]	1	0.3[6]	0.3[6]	0	0.42

Notes: [a] Scoring criteria: 1 = Yes; 0.5 = Yes, with some restrictions; 0.3 = Yes, with significant restrictions; 0 = No.
[b] The values in this column represent the mean value of the previous columns.
[1] Local discretion.
[2] With restrictions.
[3] If there is no alternative available.
[4] If child is under six months.
[5] If child is under five.
[6] Recipients with caring responsibilities can reduce the amount of work they are expected to perform.

Looking at Table 5.2, it can be observed that most schemes allow recipients to participate in education and training courses. Nonetheless, the RMI in France, SWA in Ireland and JSA in the UK do deny entitlement to individuals in full-time education (Eardley et al, 1996b, p 215; Ditch and Roberts, 2000, p 21; Guibentif and Bouget (1997), French questionnaire). There are also significant restrictions to recipients who want to provide childcare. The RMI in France and SWA in Ireland do not make any exceptions for individuals with childcare responsibilities (Eardley et al, 1996b, p 216; Enjolras et al, 2001, pp 50-1; Gautrat et al, 2000, pp 11-13). In other cases, like the RMG in Portugal,[3] SB in Denmark and TTK in Finland, recipients are only allowed to care for their children when there are no alternative forms of provision (Heikkila and Keskitalo, 2000, p 34; Rosdahl and Weise, 2001, p 171).

Table 5.2 also shows that there are important constraints on the possibility of providing care to sick or old family members. The BSHG in Germany is the only case where recipients are excused from job-search when they have dependent adults in the family (Eardley et al, 1996, p 164; Voges et al, 2001, p 78). In the case of RMG in Portugal, this is an option only when there are no alternative forms of provision.[4] JSA recipients with care responsibilities are entitled to reduce the minimum amount of hours of work they are expected to perform (16 hours per week, compared with 40 hours per week for all other recipients) (European Employment Observatory, 1999). Finally, no scheme allows recipients to perform unpaid work in social economy organisations as an alternative to paid employment.[5]

Freedom to choose a job

The other situation where recipients face a direct constraint on their ability to choose the best way to exploit their talents concerns their freedom to choose the job that they would like to do. Some schemes require recipients to accept the first job offer that they receive. Others give some leeway for recipients to choose the job that suits their abilities, experience or qualification.[6] This can be measured in terms of the possibility for recipients to refuse a job that does not match their previous occupation or their level of qualification (see Standing, 2000, p 20; Bloom and Michalopoulos, 2001, p 14).

As Table 5.3 shows, minimum income schemes put significant restrictions on recipients' freedom to choose the job they envisage as the best way to exploit their talents. The SWA in Ireland, despite being very much work-oriented, allows individuals to refuse jobs that do not match their qualifications or previous job experience.[7] The TTK in Finland, RMG in Portugal, RMI in France and SB in Denmark, on the other hand, do not consider any kind of exceptions to the obligation to accept work if offered. Nonetheless, in Denmark there is a general requirement that social workers do not force individuals into jobs that are not adjusted to their characteristics or situation (Rosdahl and Weise, 2001, p 167).

Table 5.3: Freedom to choose a job

	Justifiable excuses for job refusal		Freedom to choose the job one wants $(\sum/2)^b$
	Level of qualification[a]	Previous job[a]	
De – BSHG97	0	1	0.50
De – BSHG99	0	1	0.50
Dk – SB97	0	0	0.00
Dk – SB98	0	0	0.00
NL – ABW97	0.5[1]	0	0.25
NL – ABW99	0.5[1]	0	0.25
Fr – RMI98	0	0	0.00
Pt – RMG98	0	0	0.00
Irl – SWA98	1	1	1.00
Fin – TTK97	0	0	0.00
Fin – TTK99	0	0	0.00
UK – JSA97	0	1	0.50
UK – JSA99	0	1	0.50

Notes:
[a] Scoring criteria: 1 = Yes; 0.5 = Yes, with some restrictions; 0.3 = Yes, with significant restrictions; 0 = No.
[b] The values in this column represent the mean value of the previous columns.
[1] Only for individuals with higher qualifications.

Table 5.3 also shows that national authorities tend to judge an individual's previous occupation, more than the level of qualification, as a valid motive for refusing a job. This is the case with BSHG in Germany, SWA in Ireland and JSA in the UK, where recipients can refuse a job on the grounds that it does not allow them to pursue their previous occupation (see Eardley et al, 1996b, p 216; Ditch and Roberts, 2000, p 22; Voges et al, 2001, p 78). The SWA in Ireland and ABW in the Netherlands are the only schemes that allow individuals to refuse a job that does not match their level of qualification. Nonetheless, in the latter case, this only applies to individuals with higher qualifications, and only for a period of two years (see Eardley et al, 1996b, p 216; van Oorschot and Engelfriet, 1999, p 15; Spies and van Berkel, 2001, p 109).

Freedom from discretion

As mentioned earlier, the freedom of individuals to exploit their talents is also limited by indirect constraints, that is, mechanisms that might indirectly condition or influence a person's choice over the best way to exploit her talents (see Chapter Three). In this particular context, this refers to recipients' ability to exert their rights and choices in their relation with the bureaucratic structures that secure the implementation of minimum income schemes. To a certain point, this depends on the existence of a right of appeal from administrative decisions or on the possibility of recipients' participation in the decision-making bodies that secure the implementation of minimum income schemes.

However, the most relevant aspect here concerns the level of discretion enjoyed by social workers in their interactions with minimum income recipients. Although there are those, such as Titmuss (1971), who argue that obedience to rigid rules and procedures ignores the intensity of different needs of individuals, one should bear in mind the fact that, as Davies argues (1971), discretion opens room for arbitrariness, inequality and dependency in the relationship between recipients and social workers (see Adler and Asquith, 1981, p 11), and therefore constitutes a fundamental threat to recipients' ability to choose the best way to exploit their talents.

Unfortunately, there are important gaps in the information on the level of discretion enjoyed by social workers (see Trickey, 2001, pp 276-8). However, Trickey suggests that this might be related to the level of decentralisation in the structures that secure the implementation of minimum income schemes. In her analysis of social assistance schemes in Europe, she shows that more decentralised schemes, such as in Norway and Germany, tend to be more discretionary. In contrast, more centralised schemes, such as in the UK and the Netherlands, allow for less discretion (2000, pp 265-6, 276). In light of this, the level of discretion can be derived from the level of decentralisation of the structures that secure the implementation of minimum income schemes. This can be measured in terms of the division of funding responsibilities between central and regional/local authorities, and the decentralisation of benefit administration, namely the decisions concerning the bestowal, or termination, of benefit (see Trickey, 2001, p 266).

As can be seen in Table 5.4, the JSA in the UK and SWA in Ireland are delivered through a centralised structure of implementation, led by the (former) Department of Social Security (now the Department for Work and Pensions) in the British case, and the Department for Social, Community and Family Affairs in the Irish case. Therefore, it could be expected that these are the schemes where recipients' rights are more institutionalised. On the other hand, the TTK in Finland, SB in Denmark and BSHG in Germany are cases where the implementation of minimum income schemes is most dependent on local authorities and, therefore, there are more constraints to recipients' freedom to choose the best way to exploit their talents.

Table 5.4 also provides some interesting information about the different arrangements in the provision of the right to a minimum income. For instance, there is a significant variation in the division of funding responsibilities between central government and local authorities. In the Netherlands, local authorities are expected to fund only 10% of the costs of delivery of ABW. In Finland, on the other hand, local authorities are expected to cover around 70% of the expenses associated with the implementation of TTK. In Denmark, the funding SB is shared

Table 5.4: Freedom from discretion

	Centralisation of funding responsibilities[a]	Centralisation of benefit administration[b]	Freedom from discretion $(\sum/2)^c$
De – BSHG97	0.2[1]	0	0.10
De – BSHG99	0.2[1]	0	0.10
Dk – SB97	0.6[1]	0	0.30
Dk – SB98	0.6[1]	0	0.30
NL – ABW97	0.8[1]	0	0.40
NL – ABW99	0.8[1]	0	0.40
Fr – RMI98	1[1]	0.5	0.75
Pt – RMG98	1[1]	0.5	0.75
Irl – SWA98	1[1]	1	1.00
Fin – TTK97	0.4[2]	0	0.20
Fin – TTK99	0.4[2]	0	0.20
UK – JSA97	1[1]	1	1.00
UK – JSA99	1[1]	1	1.00

Notes:
[a] Scoring criteria: 1 = Central government funds 100% of total implementation costs; 0.8 = Central government funds between 75% and 99% of total implementation costs; 0.6 = Central government funds between 50% and 74% of total implementation costs; 0.4 = Central government funds between 25% and 49% of total implementation costs; 0.2 = Central government funds less than 25% of total implementation costs; 0 = Local authorities fund 100% of total implementation costs.
[b] Scoring criteria: 1 = Central government agencies are responsible for benefit administration; 0.5 = Benefit administration depends on multilayered structures of implementation; 0 = Local authorities are responsible for delivery.
[c] The values in this column represent the average value of the previous columns.
[1] Values refer to 1997 (see Commission of the European Communities, 1998b).
[2] Values refer to 1996 (see Commission of the European Communities, 1998b).

in equal parts by the central government and local authorities. In Germany, local authorities cover 75% of the implementation costs of BSHG. The remaining costs are allocated to the regional authorities (Länder).

Three models of benefit administration can also be identified. In the first group, which includes JSA in the UK and SWA in Ireland, the benefit is administered by central government agencies (see Eardley et al, 1996, p 214; Ditch and Roberts, 2000, p 17). The second group includes TTK in Finland, SB in Denmark, BSHG in Germany and ABW in the Netherlands, where local authorities are responsible for the administration of benefits (see Ditch et al, 1997, p 30; OECD, 1998, p 161; Hanesh and Baltzer, 2000, p 18; Oxford Research, 2000, p 25).

In the third group, which includes RMI in France and RMG in Portugal, the benefit administration is based on articulation between central government agencies and local implementation bodies. For instance, in France, the decisions on the eligibility of applicants and the payment of benefit are made by the *Caisse d'Allocations Familiales*, a nationwide body. However, the termination of benefit is dependent on a decision of the Local Insertion Committee, which comprises regional and local authorities, representatives from central government departments and a number of local stakeholders (Gautrat et al, 2000, pp 13-16). In Portugal, the Regional Social Security Commissions, which are part of the Ministry of Solidarity and Social Security, determine the eligibility of applicants and the payment of the benefit. However, as in the French scheme, the termination of benefit is dependent on a decision of the Local Support Committees, which comprises representatives from local authorities, central government departments and local stakeholders (Capucha, 1998, p 34).

Additional opportunities to work

As discussed earlier, the possibility for personal development depends not only on the possibility of choosing the best way to exploit one's talents, but on the effective opportunity to put those talents to use. In the context of the activation of minimum income recipients, this refers to the state's efforts to create additional opportunities to work and to participate in education/training courses.[8] Ideally, this should be measured by comparing the (Purchasing Power Parities-adjusted) level of expenditure on activation per minimum income recipient in the various schemes. Unfortunately, as there is no sufficient information on the number of minimum income recipients participating in ALMP, or on the expenditure used on the activation of minimum income recipients, this option was abandoned. Another possible alternative would be to compare the ratio between the level of public expenditure on passive and active unemployment policies. However, as this would be influenced by the relative share of minimum income beneficiaries in the whole unemployed population, this option was also abandoned.

In light of this, the best option is to measure the governments' efforts to create additional opportunities to work and to participate in education/training courses via the level of public expenditure in ALMP as a percentage of GDP. Although this measure is not able to capture the relationship between the level of investment and the number of minimum income recipients participating in ALMP, it is nonetheless able to measure to what degree the investment in the creation of opportunities for unemployed people is a political priority in the cases under analysis.

In the context of the creation of opportunities to work this will cover public expenditure on:

- direct job creation programmes, that is, programmes that create additional jobs for long-term unemployed people or other hard-to-employ people, and where the majority of labour costs are covered by public finances;
- employment incentives, that is, programmes that facilitate the recruitment of hard-to-employ persons, or target specific groups, and where the majority of

labour costs are covered by the employer. This can include both recruitment incentives and employment maintenance incentives;

- start–up incentives, that is, programmes that help unemployed people to create their own business or become self-employed. Assistance may take the form of loans, bursaries, provision of facilities, or advice and training in business management;
- job rotation and job sharing programmes, that is, programmes that facilitate the creation of jobs for unemployed people by replacing an employed person for a fixed period (job rotation), or by partially substituting an employed person for a limited number of working hours (job sharing) (Eurostat, 2000, pp 9-11).

As can be seen in Table 5.5, the SWA in Ireland and SB in Denmark are schemes that provide more work opportunities for minimum income recipients. France and Germany should also be noticed for their level of investment in the creation of work opportunities. The JSA in the UK and, to a lesser degree, the RMG in Portugal, are schemes where there is less effort by the public authorities to create additional work opportunities for unemployed people. Nonetheless, the introduction of the New Deal programmes in the UK did produce an increase in work opportunities for JSA recipients. The same appears to have happened in Germany, with the introduction of the 1998 Social Code, and in the Netherlands, with the introduction of the 1998 Jobseekers Employment Act.

With the exception of the Danish SB, where public authorities focus more closely on the use of employment incentives, most schemes privilege direct job creation programmes as a form of creating work opportunities for minimum income recipients. There are nonetheless significant variations in the strategies adopted by policy makers. For instance, in the Finnish case, although the majority of public expenditure goes to direct job creation programmes, there is a significant level of investment in job sharing/job rotation programmes. The SWA in Ireland, SB in Denmark and BSHG in Germany, on the other hand, make a significant investment in start–up incentives.

Opportunity to participate in education and training

In line with the previous section, recipients' opportunity to participate in education/training[9] can be measured by the level of public expenditure, as a percentage of GDP, on:

- training programmes, that is, publicly funded programmes that involve some kind of formalised instruction and are aimed at improving the employability of unemployed individuals (and other groups);
- special support for apprenticeships, that is, incentives for employers to recruit apprentices, or any form of training/apprenticeship allowance for disadvantaged groups (Eurostat, 2000, pp 8-9).

Table 5.5: Additional opportunities to work

	Expenditure on direct job creation as % of GDP	Expenditure on employment incentives as % of GDP	Expenditure on start-up incentives as % of GDP	Expenditure on job share/rotation as % of GDP	Additional opportunities to work	
					Σ^a	% of max[b]
De – BSHG97[4]	0.319[1]	0.060[1]	0.033[1]	0.000[1,3]	0.412	0.60
De – BSHG99[4]	0.350	0.080	0.038	0.000[3]	0.468	0.68
Dk – SB97	0.161[1]	0.454[1]	0.042[1]	0.003[1]	0.660	0.96
Dk – SB98	0.161	0.454	0.042	0.003	0.660	0.96
NL – ABW97	0.315[2]	0.048[1]	0.000[1,3]	0.000[2]	0.363	0.53
NL – ABW99	0.315	0.069	0.000[3]	0.000[3]	0.384	0.56
Fr – RMI98	0.307	0.189	0.001	0.000[3]	0.497	0.72
Pt – RMG98	0.056	0.043[2]	0.029	0.000[3]	0.128	0.19
Irl – SWA98	0.506	0.123	0.057	0.000	0.686	1.00
Fin – TTK97	0.250[1]	0.062[1]	0.017[1]	0.061[1]	0.390	0.57
Fin – TTK99	0.183	0.106	0.014	0.063	0.366	0.53
UK – JSA97	0.000[1,3]	0.000[1]	0.000[1]	0.000[1,3]	0.000	0.00
UK – JSA99	0.014	0.006	0.000	0.000[3]	0.020	0.03

Notes:
[a] The values in this column represent the sum of the values of the previous columns.
[b] The values in this column represent the ratio between the total investment in this case and the total investment in best performing case.
[1] Information not available. This refers to nearest neighbour, ie, 1998.
[2] Information not available. This refers to nearest neighbour, ie, 1999.
[3] Not applicable; real zero; zero by default.
[4] Given the restrictions on the participation of BSHG recipients in ALMP targeted at unemployment insurance recipients, the expenditure in work-related programmes might not represent the opportunities available to minimum income recipients.

Source: Eurostat

Looking at Table 5.6 it can be observed that the JSA, after the introduction of the New Deal programmes, the RMG in Portugal and RMI in France, are the cases where minimum income recipients are given more opportunities to participate in training or education. The ABW in the Netherlands, on the other hand, provides the fewest opportunities for recipients to improve their human capital. In Ireland, although investment in training/education is much higher than in the Netherlands, SWA recipients still have comparatively fewer opportunities to participate in training/education opportunities than recipients in the other schemes under analysis.

As in the British case, the introduction of the new Social Code in Germany prompted an increase in the level of expenditure on training/education opportunities. On the other hand, the changes in the activation framework of TTK recipients in Finland or of ABW recipients in the Netherlands did not have a significant impact on the level of expenditure on training/education.

Finally, Table 5.6 shows that national governments tend to privilege traditional training programmes, rather than apprenticeships, as a form of creating education/training opportunities for minimum income recipients. Here, the Danish case is notable, as it puts the most effort into the provision of training opportunities for minimum income recipients. The JSA in the UK, on the other hand, is the only case where expenditure on special incentives to apprenticeships exceeds investment in general training programmes.

Use of restitutive sanctions

Having looked at recipients' freedom and opportunities to exploit their talents, we now turn to how schemes enforce their obligation to develop themselves. As mentioned earlier, the focus here will be on the restitutive/repressive character of the sanctions used in the activation of minimum income recipients. Therefore, the purpose is to determine to what degree the sanctions regime imposed on minimum income recipients are designed to induce recipients to comply with the activation requirement that is attached to the right to a minimum income, rather than simply punish them for failing to comply with their obligations (see Chapter Three).

This can be measured by looking at three different aspects of the sanctions regime imposed on minimum income recipients (see Saunders et al, 2001, p 50; Trickey, 2001, p 277):[10]

- the possibility of cancelling the entitlement to minimum income protection in case of infringement;
- the maximum penalty in the case of a first infringement;
- the use of progressive sanctions, that is, the use of harsher penalties as recipients continue to fail to fulfil their obligations.

Table 5.6: Opportunity to participate in education and training

	Expenditure on training as % of GDP	Expenditure on special support for apprenticeship as % of GDP	Opportunity to participate in education and training	
			Σ^a	% of max[b]
De – BSHG97[3]	0.389[1]	0.045[1]	0.434	0.61
De – BSHG99[3]	0.411	0.058	0.469	0.66
Dk – SB97	0.693[2]	0.015[2]	0.708	1.00
Dk – SB98	0.693	0.015	0.708	1.00
NL – ABW97	0.055[1]	0.040[1]	0.095	0.13
NL – ABW99	0.064	0.038	0.102	0.14
Fr – RMI98	0.318	0.102	0.420	0.59
Pt – RMG98	0.174	0.065	0.239	0.34
Irl – SWA98	0.223	0.000	0.223	0.31
Fin – TTK97	0.489[1]	0.044[1]	0.533	0.75
Fin – TTK99	0.450	0.035	0.485	0.69
UK – JSA97	0.039[1]	0.099[1]	0.138	0.19
UK – JSA99	0.046	0.106	0.152	0.21

Notes:
[a] The values in this column represent the sum of the values of the previous columns.
[b] The values in this column represent the ratio between the total investment in this case and the total investment in best performing case.
[1] Data refer to 1998.
[2] Data refer to 1999.
[3] Given the restrictions on the participation of BSHG recipients in ALMP targeted at unemployment insurance recipients, the expenditure in training and education programmes might not represent the opportunities available to minimum income recipients.

Source: Eurostat

In line with the distinction between repressive and restitutuive sanctions put forward earlier, it can be assumed that schemes where the enforcement of sanctions may involve cancelling entitlement to minimum income protection, that impose harsher penalties in the case of a first infringement, and that do not use progressive sanctions, tend to emphasise the repressive character of sanctions. On the other hand, schemes where the enforcement of sanctions does not entail cancelling entitlement to minimum income protection, that impose milder penalties in the case of a first infringement, and that use progressive sanctions, tend to emphasise the restitutive character of sanctions.

As Table 5.7 demonstrates, the BSHG in Germany and ABW in the Netherlands are the closest to the ideal-type of restitutive sanctions. In none of these cases can the application of benefit sanctions lead to the cessation of entitlement rights. There is also a preoccupation in using progressive sanctions to enforce the obligations of recipients. The most repressive schemes, on the other hand, are RMI in France, RMG in Portugal, JSA in the UK and SB in Denmark, before the introduction of the 1998 Act of Active Social Policy. In the French case, recipients who fail to comply with the insertion contract, or fail to come to all three evaluation interviews, can have their benefit suspended, or even cancelled (Lefevre and Zoyem, 1999, p 2). In Portugal, any RMG recipients who fail to comply with the activities agreed in the insertion contract will have their benefit cancelled (Capucha, 1998, p 40; Cardoso and Ramos, 2000, p 15). Before the introduction of the 1998 Act of Active Social Policy, although there was no specific obligation to look for a job, all SB recipients who refused an activation offer from the local authorities could lose their entitlement to minimum income (Eardley et al, 1996b, p 115). After 1998, the sanction was transformed into a 20% cut in their benefit (Kildal, 2001, p 8).

As Table 5.7 also shows, the SWA in Ireland, RMG in Portugal and RMI in France are the schemes that apply the most severe sanctions to first-time transgressors. As seen earlier, in the French and Portuguese cases, a first infringement can lead to the end of entitlement. In the Irish case, an initial infraction can lead to the suspension of benefit for up to nine weeks (Eardley et al, 1996b, p 150). The JSA in the UK also imposes a harsh penalty for first-time offenders. Thus JSA recipients who fail to attend a job interview, to participate in a 'New Deal option' or to follow a 'jobseeker's direction',[11] will receive a fixed a two-week benefit suspension (Trickey and Walker, 2001, pp 201-2). In the remaining countries, the sanction for a first infringement is significantly lower. In Germany, BSHG recipients who refuse a job offer for the first time are subject to a sanction of up to 25% of the standard rate of benefit (Voges et al, 2001, pp 86-7). In the Netherlands, a first infringement will be sanctioned with a 5%-20% benefit reduction (van Oorschot and Engelfriet, 1999, p 15).

Looking at Table 5.7 it can be observed that most of the cases under analysis use progressive sanctions to enforce recipients' obligations. In the UK, any further transgressions after a first sanction are punished with a four-week benefit suspension (Trickey and Walker, 2001, pp 201-2). In the Netherlands, continuous non-conformity can lead to the full withdrawal of benefit for a month (van Oorschot and Engelfriet, 1999, p 15). In Germany, BSHG recipients who, after the imposition of a first sanction, fail to fulfil their obligations can have their share of household benefit removed (Voges et al, 2001, pp 86-7). In contrast, the Danish SB (before the introduction of the 1998 Act of Active Social Policy), the RMG in Portugal and RMI in France do not use progressive sanctions.

The introduction of the 1998 Social Assistance Act reduced the repressive character of the sanctions regime by introducing progressive sanctions. Thus, whereas prior to 1998 recipients who continuously failed to comply with the activation requirements were subject to a fixed 20% cut in their benefit, from 1998 onwards, these infringements were punished with a harsher penalty – a 40% benefit reduction (Heikkila and Keskitalo, 1999, pp 15-16; 2000, p 34).

Table 5.7: Use of restitutive sanctions

	Possibility of cancellation of benefit (0.5)[a,b]	Maximum sanction for first infringement (0.25)[a]		Use of progressive sanctions (0.25)[a,e,f]	Use of restitutive sanctions Σ[g]
		Maximum sanction as a percentage of the monthly amount of benefit[a,c]	Score[d]		
De – BSHG97	1	25%	0.75	1	0.94
De – BSHG99	1	25%	0.75	1	0.94
Dk – SB97	0	100%	0	0	0.00
Dk – SB98	1	20%	1	0	0.75
NL – ABW97	1	20%	1	1	1.00
NL – ABW99	1	20%	1	1	1.00
Fr – RMI98	0	100%	0	0	0.00
Pt – RMG98	0	100%	0	0	0.00
Irl – SWA98	1	100%	0	1	0.75
Fin – TTK97	1	20%	1	0	0.75
Fin – TTK99	1	20%	1	1	1.00
UK – JSA97	0	50%	0.5	1	0.38
UK – JSA99	0	50%	0.5	1	0.38

Notes:
[a] This excludes sanctions related to the non-signature of an Insertion Contract/Jobseeker's Agreement or the provision of false information concerning the recipient's financial situation.
[b] Scoring criteria: 1 = No; 0 = Yes.
[c] Scoring criteria: Given the great variation in the sanction regimes under analysis, this indicator was standardised according the following rules:
* when the sanctions are defined as a full suspension of weekly benefit, it will be assumed that this corresponds to 25% of the monthly benefit;
* when the maximum penalty is the cancellation of benefit, it will be assumed that this corresponds to 100% of monthly benefit;
* in cases where there are differentiated sanctions for different infractions, the value will reflect the maximum penalty for the minor infraction(s).
[d] Scoring criteria: 1 = Sanction represents less than 25% of monthly amount of benefit; 0.75 = Sanction represents between 25% and 49% of monthly amount of benefit; 0.50 = Sanction represents between 50% and 74% of monthly amount of benefit; 0.25 = Sanction represents between 75% and 99% of monthly amount of benefit; 0 = Sanction represents 100% of monthly amount of benefit.
[e] Scoring criteria: 1 = Yes; 0 = No.
[f] In cases where schemes set a maximum level of sanction, and then let social workers to use their discretion to determine the level of sanction that is appropriate, it will be assumed that progressive sanctions are in use.
[g] The values in this column represent the weighted sum of the values of the previous columns.

Index of respect for the right to personal development

Having identified the institutional features that best capture the schemes' respect for the right to personal development this comparative exercise can be concluded by examining how the schemes are positioned with regards to an index of respect for the right to personal development. However, this will be conditioned by two factors. The first concerns the possible bias associated with the problems experienced in the measurement of recipients' opportunity to work and to participate in education/training.

The second concerns the distribution of weights between the various indicators. As can be seen in Table 5.8, this reflects the logical priority between the different dimensions of the normative framework (see Chapter Three). For instance, in acknowledging the importance of satisfying the basic consumption needs of individuals as a fundamental condition for exercise of individual freedoms, opportunities and obligations, this dimension will receive a higher weight in the index. In the same way, acknowledging the requirement that there should be a balance between recipients' rights and responsibilities, the index attributes the same weight to the use of restitutive sanctions as it does to the institutional features that measure recipients' freedom and opportunities to exploit their talents. As a consequence of this, the schemes' final position in the index might be overly influenced by how they score with regard to the recipients' disposable income or the restitutive character of the sanctions regime.

As Table 5.8 shows, the ABW in the Netherlands is the scheme that shows the highest respect for the right of recipients to personal development. In Denmark, the introduction of the 1998 Act of Active Social Policy had a significant impact on the scheme's position, making it one of the cases with the highest respect for the right to personal development. In contrast, the RMI in France and RMG in Portugal are the schemes that least respect recipients' right to personal development. The JSA in the UK also occupies a lower position in the index.

In the same way as in Denmark, the introduction of the 1998 Social Assistance Act in Finland, as it established a more progressive sanctions regime, also had a positive impact on the schemes' position in the index. Had the level of benefit not been reduced in that same period, the impact would surely be even more visible. In the UK and Germany, changes in the activation framework of minimum income recipients also had a positive, albeit small, impact on the scheme's position in the index.

Table 5.8: Index of respect for the right to personal development

	Satisfaction of basic consumption needs (*0.4)	Freedom to take other activities instead of paid work (*0.05)	Freedom to choose type of job (*0.05)	Freedom from discretion (*0.05)	Additional opportunities to work (*0.075)	Opportunity to participate in education and training (*0.075)	Use of restitutive sanctions (*0.3)	Respect for the right to personal development[a]
De – BSHG97	0.52	0.60	0.50	0.10	0.60	0.61	0.94	0.64
De – BSHG99	0.52	0.60	0.50	0.10	0.68	0.66	0.94	0.64
Dk – SB97	0.85	0.50	0.00	0.30	0.96	1.00	0.00	0.51
Dk – SB98	0.89	0.50	0.00	0.30	0.96	1.00	0.75	0.77
NL – ABW97	0.97	0.60	0.25	0.40	0.53	0.13	1.00	0.78
NL – ABW99	0.96	0.60	0.25	0.40	0.56	0.14	1.00	0.77
Fr – RMI98	0.61	0.30	0.00	0.75	0.72	0.59	0.00	0.36
Pt – RMG98	0.52	0.60	0.00	0.75	0.19	0.34	0.00	0.33
Irl – SWA98	0.73	0.30	1.00	1.00	1.00	0.31	0.75	0.63
Fin – TTK97	0.68	0.50	0.00	0.20	0.57	0.75	0.75	0.62
Fin – TTK99	0.62	0.50	0.00	0.20	0.53	0.69	1.00	0.69
UK – JSA97	0.58	0.12	0.50	1.00	0.00	0.19	0.38	0.39
UK – JSA99	0.59	0.42	0.50	1.00	0.03	0.21	0.38	0.41

Notes:
[a] The values in this column represent the weighted sum of the values of the previous columns.

Conclusion

This concludes the first analysis of the relationship between the employment effectiveness of minimum income schemes and their respect for the right to a minimum income. Going through the various dimensions that operationalise this normative framework, this chapter has shown that ABW in the Netherlands is the scheme that scores highest in the index of respect for the right to personal development. In contrast, the RMI in France and RMG in Portugal are the schemes with the least respect.

When looking at the various dimensions of the respect for the right to personal development, the chapter has shown that ABW in the Netherlands and SB in Denmark are schemes where recipients' disposable income is closer to the poverty line. Concerning recipients' freedom to exploit their talents, the chapter has also shown that RMG in Portugal, BSHG in Germany and ABW in the Netherlands are schemes where minimum income recipients have more freedom to choose other activities instead of paid employment. On the other hand, SWA in Ireland is the only scheme that allows individuals to refuse jobs that do not match their qualifications or previous job experience. JSA in the UK and SWA in Ireland, as they depend on very centralised structures of implementation, are the schemes where recipients are freer from the discretionary power of social workers.

Regarding recipients' opportunities to exploit their talents, the chapter has shown that SWA in Ireland and SB in Denmark are the schemes recipients have more additional opportunities to work. On the other hand, RMG in Portugal, RMI in France and JSA in the UK (after the introduction of the New Deal programmes) are the cases where minimum income recipients have been given more opportunities to participate in training or education. Finally, the chapter has shown that BSHG in Germany and ABW in the Netherlands are the schemes that are closer to the ideal-type of restitutive sanctions.

Notes

[1] The household's disposable income is the product of the sum of the value of the minimum income benefit and Family Allowances, subtracted by the amount of benefit subject to taxation (where applicable). For further details see Appendix A to this volume.

[2] In order to improve comparability between the different cases, this was calculated for four different households, and then an average value was derived. For further details see Appendix A to this volume.

[3] Decree 196-A/97.

[4] Decree 196-A/97.

[5] In the UK, JSA recipients are allowed to perform voluntary work with not-for-profit or non-governmental organisations. However, the recipient will be expected to continue to actively look for work and be available to attend an interview within 48 hours and take up work within one week (see Statutory Instrument 1996, No 207, Chapter II – Availability for employment, retrieved from www.opsi.gov.uk/si/si1996/Uksi_19960207_en_3.htm#mdiv5).

[6] In some countries, such as the UK (see Ditch and Roberts, 2000, p 22), recipients can refuse a job on the grounds that it pays less than their previous job. However, as the right to choose the best way to exploit one's talents refers to the type of jobs one can perform, rather than the rate of pay one can receive, this option will not be included in this analysis.

[7] The Social Welfare (Consolidation) Act of 1993 (section 120), retrieved from www.irishstatutebook.ie/ZZA27Y1993.html

[8] This poses a secondary problem, which cannot be dealt with here, regarding the quality of the opportunities offered to minimum income recipients. If a training or a job creation programme is badly designed and does not really contribute to participants' personal development, then one can question if it is sufficient to look at the amount invested in the activation of minimum income recipients.

[9] Unfortunately, there are no specific data for the measurement of recipients' opportunities to participate in education courses. One option would be to look at the level of expenditure on institutional training, which refers to programmes where more than 75% of training time is spent in training institutions, such as schools/colleges or training centres (Eurostat, 2000, pp 8-9). Yet, the Eurostat does not provide information on this sub-category. In light of this, it was decided to use the expenditure on training and special support for apprenticeships as a proxy indicator of the opportunities of minimum income recipients to engage in education.

[10] Alternatively, other indicators could be used, such as the use of family sanctions, or the curtailment of future entitlement rights. However, as these are marginal elements in the activation of minimum income recipients in the European context, it was decided to exclude them from the analysis.

[11] When recipients refuse to attend any of the opportunities offered by the New Deal, they can be issued with a Jobseeker's direction, which defines the guidelines concerning job-search, or the attendance of New Deal options (Trickey and Walker, 2001, p 201).

The employment effectiveness of minimum income schemes

Having measured respect for recipients' right to personal development, we now turn to the schemes' employment effectiveness. Before moving on to the analysis, we should clarify what is actually meant by employment effectiveness. As mentioned earlier (see Chapter One), activation here means a policy of combining negative and positive incentives with the purpose of helping income support recipients to become self-sufficient through paid employment. This has implications for the measurement of the employment effectiveness of minimum income schemes, in particular regarding the treatment of subsidised work, which cannot be considered to represent a fully self-sufficient form of existence for recipients. In light of this, employment effectiveness here will refer to the schemes' ability to place recipients in unsubsidised employment.

The story so far

Going through the European literature on the activation of minimum income recipients it can be observed that the existing studies have focused more on the effectiveness of the activation of specific recipient groups, and specific activation programmes, than on the overall employment effectiveness of minimum income schemes. For instance, in Denmark, Ingerslev (1994) found that 50% of social assistance beneficiaries who participated in activation programmes (Youth Benefit Scheme and the Municipal Employment Act) started work or education (see Dahl and Pedersen, 2002, p 4). In 1997, Weise and Brogaard (1997) found that participation in activation increased the employment rate of beneficiaries from 12% to 15% (see Pedersen et al, 2002, pp 11-12). In Norway, Lorentzen and Dahl found that the participation in active labour market policy (ALMP), especially packages that combine wage subsides and training, improves the minimum income recipients' chances of going into work (2005, pp 35-40).

Nonetheless, there have been some attempts to evaluate the effectiveness of minimum income schemes. In France, Cordazzo (1999) found that in 1995, 24% of a sample of individuals who entered the RMI scheme within the Department of Gironde in 1989 had entered employment (see Enjolras, 2002, p 13). Afsa and Guillemot (1999), on the other hand, found that 61% of people leaving the RMI scheme in 1997 gained a job in the labour market (see Enjolras, 2002, p 16). Demailly (1999) found that, of all households receiving RMI in January 1996, 30% had left the RMI in January 1998. More importantly, the Demailly found that 66% of the exits were due to the fact that one of the heads of household had found a job or had been enrolled in an employment programme (see Enjolras, 2002, p 15). In Portugal, an evaluation of the RMG showed that 65% of the recipients available for work (which included individuals aged between 16 and 55 and with no inhibiting health problems) succeeded in finding a job (see da Costa, 2003, p 86). In the Netherlands, a study conducted in the city of Rotterdam showed that in the period between January 2000 and April 2003, only 19.95% of the total 86,801 individuals who received social assistance during this period were able to find a job (van Berkel, 2007, p 131).

Unfortunately, these national evaluations do not provide a satisfactory pool of evidence for a comparative study of the employment effectiveness of minimum income schemes in Europe. Not only that, as Dahl and Pedersen rightly note (2002, pp 71-2), the available studies show a significant level of variation in terms of their understanding of employment effectiveness and the methodological approaches used to access it. So, it seems better to focus on the comparative evidence on the employment effectiveness of minimum income schemes in Europe. Unfortunately, despite all the political attention it attracted at the European level, it is only possible to identify two relevant attempts to compare the employment effectiveness of minimum income schemes in Europe.

The first of these attempts is the Commission of the European Communities' study of the effectiveness of minimum income schemes in a number of EU member countries. Using institutional/administrative data, this study suggests that the French RMI is the most effective minimum income scheme, as 27% of recipients were able to find a job. The least effective scheme, on the other hand, was the *Revenu Minimum Guaranti* in Luxembourg (Commission of the European Communities, 1998a, p 28). In Denmark and Spain, close to 15% of recipients entered the labour market. However, as can be seen from Table 6.1, this study does not differentiate between subsidised and unsubsidised employment, and therefore does not provide an accurate representation of the employment effectiveness of minimum income schemes.

The other relevant attempt was Nicaise et al's (2003) study of the insertion potential of minimum income schemes in the EU. Using data from the ECHP, Nicaise et al measured the average probability of a minimum income recipient, in any given month, being in work in the next 12 months (see Nicaise et al, 2003, Annex 7, p 76). This study suggests that Austria and Denmark, alongside Finland and Spain, are the most effective at returning minimum income recipients back into the labour market. In contrast, Ireland and Germany present the lowest levels of effectiveness (see Table 6.2).

Despite its significance, this study has some limitations. Firstly, as in the case of the study conducted by the Commission of the European Communities (1998a), the authors do not differentiate between transitions to subsidised and unsubsidised employment. Secondly, they use average yearly transition probabilities, which ignore variations in the employment effectiveness within countries. Thirdly, as they themselves admit, these 'yearly transition rates' consist of estimates, rather than actual transitions between states. Therefore, it is impossible to determine whether

Table 6.1: Results achieved by socioeconomic integration measures (% of total recipients)

	Activated	No longer receiving minimum income	Employ-ment	Unpaid work	Training	Other
Denmark	49	20-30	15	–	34	50[1]
Germany	8.4	–	–	–	–	–
Spain	100[2]	–	13[3]	na	na	0.05[4]
France	28	33	27	–	6	52[9]
Luxembourg	12.0	6.0[5]	4.7	3.9	3.5	79.5[6]
Netherlands	–	32.9	11.6	na	0.6	18.8[7]
Portugal	21.8	–	9.7	–	21.5	50.1[8]

Notes: – = No information given; na = Not available.
[1] In supplement to other benefits.
[2] In theory.
[3] Protected employment.
[4] Social integration projects (healthcare, children's education, etc).
[5] In 1996.
[6] Exempt from additional social measures
[7] Of which four have moved abroad; four marriages.
[8] 18.6, healthcare; 23.7, social support; 7.8, housing.
[9] Of which 47 jobseekers.

Source: Adapted from Commission of the European Communities (1998a, p 28)

they over-estimate or under-estimate the schemes' employment effectiveness[1] (Nicaise et al, 2003, Annex 7, p 76).

Finally, Nicaise et al do not take into account the influence of labour market conditions on the effectiveness of minimum income schemes, particularly their ability to re-integrate unemployed people. For instance, Theodore and Peck (2000) argue that the relative success of workfare schemes in the US must be understood in the context of a booming economy, which was creating new jobs anyway (2000, p 87). Therefore, one would expect that more buoyant labour markets would absorb a larger share of minimum income recipients.

This seems to be confirmed by a White House Council of Economic Advisers' (1999) study that shows that in the period between 1993 and 1996, 26% to 36% of the

Table 6.2: Average yearly probabilities of transition between minimum income and work

1993-97	
Austria	45.05
Belgium	27.54
France	27.90
Germany	17.19
Luxembourg	26.02
Britain	25.52
Ireland	18.10
Denmark	45.11
Finland	39.82
Spain	34.47

Source: Nicaise et al (2003, Annex 7)

overall decline in the percentage of welfare recipients was due to improvements in the US labour market. Not only that, they show that even after the introduction of Temporary Assistance for Needy Families (TANF), which enhanced the positive and negative incentives to force recipients into the labour market, labour market conditions could still explain 8% to 10% of the overall decline in welfare caseloads (Council of Economic Advisers, 1999, p 23).

This is further confirmed by Cornilleau et al's (2000) study of the effect of employment growth on RMI caseloads in France. According to the authors (2000, p 7), during the period between 1997 and 1999, the creation of 870,000 jobs contributed to a reduction of approximately 5% in the RMI recipient population. However, these results must be taken with caution. First, these studies fail to differentiate between entries and departures from social assistance. Second, and most importantly, they fail to differentiate between the overall reduction in recipient welfare caseloads and the number of recipients who found a job.

Despite its limitations, the study carried out by Nicaise et al (2003) does provide clear indications as to the most appropriate way to carry this study forward. The first indication is that the best option to measure the employment effectiveness of minimum income schemes is to look at the beneficiaries' transitions from minimum income to unsubsidised work. The ECHP, as it provides comparable data on the labour force status and sources of income of respondents, provides the necessary data to measure those transitions.

However, in order to avoid the problems identified in average yearly transition probabilities used by Nicaise et al (2003), the best option is to look at the percentage of minimum income recipients who, within a year, make the transition to unsubsidised work. It should be recognised that, as it does not measure transitions that occur in a shorter period of time, this indicator might under-estimate the schemes' employment effectiveness. However, as it is based on effective rather than estimated transitions, it provides a clearer and more adequate measure of the scheme's effectiveness.

The second indication is that it is not enough to measure the percentage of minimum income recipients who make the transition to work. Bearing in mind that the differences between the various cases can be justified by differences in existing labour market conditions, it is necessary to devise a measure of employment effectiveness that cancels differences in labour markets' ability to re-integrate unemployed people.

Measuring transitions from minimum income to work

So, the first step in this endeavour is to use ECHP micro-data to measure the percentage of minimum income recipients who, within a year, make the transition to unsubsidised work. However, as one would expect, not all minimum income recipients can be included in this analysis. For instance, there are individuals who are entitled to social assistance benefits, but only as a supplement to unemployment benefits. This would cause a problem in the later stages of analysis as individuals' transitions are conditioned not by the rules that regulate the right to a minimum income, but by those that regulate the ascription of unemployment benefits. Therefore, in order to avoid this, it is better to exclude individuals receiving any type of unemployment benefits from this analysis.

A second problem concerns the availability to work of individuals who receive minimum income benefits. Given its role in providing a safety-net to all people in society, minimum income schemes include a variety of groups with different levels of job readiness. This could produce a bias against those schemes with the highest percentage of recipients who are not available for work. In light of this, it is advisable to exclude from this analysis all recipients doing housework, looking after children (which does not necessarily exclude all women with childcare responsibilities) or dependent adults, in retirement, or economically inactive.

A third issue that needs to be taken into consideration concerns those individuals who, while receiving minimum income benefit, are in training/education, in an apprenticeship or in a job creation scheme. This is especially problematic concerning individuals in apprenticeships or job creation schemes, as some could argue that they are no longer minimum income recipients. However, as stated earlier, employment effectiveness here refers to transitions into unsubsidised employment. The assumption here is that even if these individuals are in work, this should be seen as part of the activation process that is enforced on all minimum income beneficiaries. Therefore, it seems only right to include them in this study.

In addition to the problems related to the specificities of the minimum income population, the limitations imposed by ECHP to this study should also be borne in mind. For instance, given the subsidiary role of minimum income schemes in social protection systems and the attrition effects characteristic of panel data, there will be a small number of observations for analysis.[2] Of course, this raises issues about reliability. In order to avoid this problem, in line with the criterion adopted by Lehmann and Wirtz (2004, p 7), only cases with more than 20 observations were subject to analysis.[3]

Another relevant problem concerns the difficulties posed by ECHP to the measurement of the employment effectiveness in the British cases. As seen earlier (see Chapter Four), JSA involves both an unemployment insurance and an unemployment assistance component, which provides a safety-net for unemployed individuals. Unfortunately, ECHP does not differentiate between individuals on unemployment insurance and those on unemployment assistance (see EPUNET, 2005, p 30). In order to deal with this, it was necessary to adopt an alternative approach to the measurement of the employment effectiveness of the scheme, which limits analysis to all individuals who have been unemployed for more than six months. This limits the comparability of the English cases, as it reduces the percentage of recipients who are participating in education/training courses or in job creation schemes.

As can be seen from Table 6.3, minimum income schemes show significant shortcomings in helping recipients to gain self-sufficiency through work. In fact, on average, only a quarter of recipients were able to find work after a year on minimum income. However, one should bear in mind the possibility that the percentage of individuals in work is partly related to the percentage of people still in education, training or job creation schemes. As Table 6.3 also shows, in the period between 1997 and 1999, there is a reduction in the percentage in the Dutch and German minimum income recipients who make the transition to work, which is accompanied by an increase in the percentage of individuals in education/training/job creation.[4] The British case is more difficult to explain. Although there is a decrease in the JSA's employment effectiveness, the introduction of the New Deal programmes did not produce an increase in the 'education/training/job creation' category. This might be related with the fact that New Deal options are only expected to last six months (see Ditch and Roberts, 2000, p 33).

Looking at Table 6.3, one can observe that TTK in Finland is the scheme with the highest percentage of recipients who made the transition to work. The SB in Denmark, SWA in Ireland and JSA in the UK also present a level of effectiveness above average. In contrast, German BSHG (especially after the introduction of the 1998 Social Code), Dutch ABW (especially after the introduction of the 1998

Table 6.3: Activity status of recipients one year after being on minimum income

	Work		In education/ training/ job creation		Unemployed		Other	
	N	%	N	%	N	%	N	%
De – BSHG97	18	21.43	23	27.38	27	32.14	16	19.05
De – BSHG99	10	14.71	26	38.24	18	26.47	14	20.58
Dk – SB97	20	29.85	27	40.30	12	17.91	8	11.94
Dk – SB98	14	28.00	23	46.00	8	16.00	5	10.00
NL – ABW97	20	20.62	21	21.65	37	38.14	19	19.59
NL – ABW99	11	15.07	23	31.51	26	35.62	13	17.80
Fr – RMI98	18	18.37	14	14.29	60	61.22	6	6.12
Pt – RMG98	9	22.50	5	12.50	18	45.00	8	20.00
Irl – SWA98	40	29.41	47	34.56	35	25.74	14	10.29
Fin – TTK97	80	35.09	82	35.96	37	16.23	29	12.72
Fin – TTK99	46	35.94	32	25.00	36	28.13	14	10.93
UK – JSA97	9	31.03	0	0.00	17	58.62	3	10.35
UK – JSA99	9	28.13	0	0.00	21	65.63	2	6.24
Σ/13[a]		25.40		25.18		35.91		13.51

Note: [a] This value represents the unweighted sum of the values for all cases in the relevant column.
Source: ECHP (1994-2001)

Jobseekers' Employment Act), the RMG in Portugal and RMI in France are the schemes that are least effective in returning recipients to the labour market.

Capturing labour market conditions

Having measured the percentage of minimum income beneficiaries who make the transitions to work, the next stage is to adjust this to the labour markets' ability to absorb unemployed people. Traditionally, the labour market literature has used the unemployment rate to capture this. However, as Schomann and Kruppe point out (1996, p 33), stock indicators such as the unemployment rate, fail to capture the dynamic processes that go on in labour markets. In this particular case, the unemployment rate hides the employment creation and destruction dynamics in labour markets.

Following Kruppe's (2001) ground-breaking work, it can be argued that a labour market's ability to create jobs for unemployed people – from here forward, unemployment reintegration capacity (URC) – can be measured by combining the information from two indicators:

- the 'inflow into dependent employment', which measures the number of individuals who have entered employment in a given year;
- the 'share of flow from unemployment in all inflows into dependent employment', which measures to what degree the creation of new jobs is based on the recruitment of unemployed individuals (see Kruppe, 2001, p 13).

As can be seen from Table 6.4, the URC indicator reflects different models of job creation. In the UK, Germany and Denmark, the labour market's URC is more related to their overall capacity to create new jobs than with the weight of the pool of unemployed in the creation of new jobs. In contrast, in France and Portugal, the labour market has a lower capacity to create new jobs, but the percentage of the new jobs that go to unemployed people is higher. The Finnish labour market is the only case that combines a high capacity of job creation and a great ability to reintegrate unemployed people back into the labour market.

However, despite the structural differences between these countries, there is little variation in their ability to create jobs for unemployed people. Finland, France and Germany are the countries where the labour markets show the best performance. The Netherlands, on the other hand, is the worst performer. Nonetheless, one should notice that, between 1997 and 1999, the Finnish, German and Dutch labour markets lost some of their capacity of creating jobs for unemployed people.

Adjusting the effectiveness of guaranteed minimum income schemes to labour markets conditions

Having analysed the ability of labour markets to reintegrate unemployed individuals, it is finally possible to adjust the employment effectiveness of the

Table 6.4: Unemployment reintegration capacity

	Inflow into employment (*0.6)[c]	% of max[a]	Share of flow from unemployment in all inflows into dependent employment (*0.4)[c]	% of max[a]	URC Σ[b]
De – BSHG97[1]	16.60	1.00	18.10	0.37	0.75
De – BSHG99[2]	15.60	0.94	16.30	0.33	0.70
Dk – SB97[1]	12.40	0.75	18.90	0.39	0.60
Dk – SB98[3]	11.50	0.69	20.70	0.42	0.59
NL – ABW97[1]	8.30	0.50	25.70	0.53	0.51
NL – ABW99[3]	7.90	0.48	22.30	0.46	0.47
Fr – RMI98[3]	9.50	0.57	48.80	1.00	0.74
Pt – RMG98[3]	8.00	0.48	36.20	0.74	0.59
Irl – SWA98[4]	11.60	0.70	29.70	0.61	0.66
Fin – TTK97[1]	13.30	0.80	35.30	0.72	0.77
Fin – TTK99[2]	12.20	0.73	32.30	0.66	0.71
UK – JSA97[1]	14.00	0.84	17.90	0.37	0.65
UK – JSA99[2]	15.10	0.91	12.80	0.26	0.65

Notes: [a] In order to standardise the data from sub-indicators that compose URC, it was decided to compare the values of each case with the best performing case.
[b] This value is the product of the weighted sum of the scores of the previous columns.
[c] The distribution of weights between the two dimensions of this indicator departs from the premise that the 'Share of flow from unemployment in all inflows into dependent employment' should have the same or a lower weight than the 'Inflow into employment'. A sensitivity analysis of the impact of different distributions of weights in a correlation between the employment effectiveness of the schemes and the URC showed that the 0.6/0.4 distribution is the one that produces the highest correlation (see Appendix B, this volume).
[1] 1998.
[2] 2000.
[3] 1999.
[4] 1997.

Source: ILO (2003)

cases under analysis. As Table 6.5 shows, there is a positive correlation between the employment effectiveness of minimum income schemes and the labour market's URC ($r = 0.34$). In light of this, it can be argued that it is possible to forecast the employment effectiveness of a given scheme for a given value of the labour market URC:

$$y' = E\,[y|x]\,. \times \{\alpha * 0.6 + \beta * 0.4\}$$

where:

y' refers to the expected value (E) of the employment effectiveness (y) for a given value of the labour market URC (x)

α refers to the value of the Inflow to dependent employment, and

β refers to the value of the share of flow from unemployment in all inflows into dependent employment

If one then subtracts the value of y by y', one can identify the scheme's marginal employment effectiveness (z), that is, the difference between the real and the expected effectiveness under the current labour market conditions:

$$z = y - y'$$

As it neutralises the impact of labour market conditions, this indicator provides the most adequate measure for the comparison of the employment effectiveness of minimum income schemes. If the value of z is positive, this means that the employment effectiveness of the scheme is, given the existing labour market conditions, higher than expected. If, on the other hand, the value of z is negative, this means the scheme is under-performing in its ability to return recipients to the labour market.

As Table 6.5 shows, even when labour market conditions are taken into account, TTK in Finland is the most effective scheme at putting recipients back into the labour market. The JSA in the UK and SB in Denmark also show a positive marginal effectiveness. In contrast, BSHG in Germany, especially after the introduction of the 1998 Social Code, and RMI in France are the schemes that are the least effective at returning recipients to the labour market. The RMG in Portugal and ABW in the Netherlands, especially after the introduction of the 1998 Jobseekers Employment Act, also show negative marginal employment effectiveness.

This also suggests that the introduction of the 1998 Social Assistance Act in Finland had a positive impact on the scheme's ability to return recipients back to the labour market. In contrast, the changes in the activation framework for BSHG, ABW and JSA recipients, rather than improving, prompted a decrease in their marginal effectiveness.[5]

Conclusion

After looking at the schemes' respect for recipients' right to personal development, this chapter then focused on their employment effectiveness. It started by looking at the percentage of minimum income recipients that, within a year, made the transition to unsubsidised work. However, as the differences between the cases under analysis could be affected by the ability of the labour markets to reintegrate unemployed people, it seemed more useful to look at the schemes' marginal

Table 6.5: Marginal effectiveness of minimum income schemes

	Minimum income employment effectiveness (Y)	URC (X)	Expected employment effectiveness (Y' = E[Y¦X])	Minimum income marginal effectiveness (Z =Y-Y')
De – BSHG97	21.43	0.75	28.08	–6.65
De – BSHG99	14.71	0.70	26.76	–12.05
Dk–- SB97	29.85	0.60	24.31	5.54
Dk – SB98	28.00	0.59	23.85	4.15
NL – ABW97	20.62	0.51	21.91	–1.29
NL – ABW99	15.07	0.47	20.82	–5.75
Fr – RMI98	18.37	0.74	27.95	–9.58
Pt – RMG98	22.50	0.59	23.86	–1.36
Irl – SWA98	29.41	0.66	25.86	3.55
Fi –TTK97	35.09	0.77	28.64	6.45
Fin –TTK99	35.94	0.71	26.97	8.97
UK – JSA97	31.03	0.65	25.60	5.43
UK – JSA99	28.13	0.65	25.55	2.58
		$r = 0.34$		

employment effectiveness, which was able to adjust the schemes' effectiveness to existing labour market conditions. In conclusion, when labour market conditions are taken into account, TTK in Finland is the most effective scheme at putting recipients back into the labour market. In contrast, BSHG in Germany, especially after the introduction of the 1998 Social Code, and RMI in France, are the least effective schemes.

Notes

[1] Another problem concerns the fact that the methodology adopted does not take into account duration effects, that is, the influence that the time spent in a given situation can have on the individual's likelihood of moving on to a different state. For instance, evidence suggests that, the longer a person has been unemployed, the less likely it is that they will find a job (Nicaise et al, 2003, Annex 7, p 76).

[2] In addition, ECHP does not present any information on the duration of the benefit episode. Hence, it is impossible to determine when the benefit episode started, or when it ended. Not only that, as with any other large-scale survey, ECHP presents some inconsistencies in the data concerning the availability of individuals for work. For instance, there were 22 respondents who a year prior to the date of the interview were in training and education but, nonetheless, said they did not attend any course during the previous year. There were also four cases of respondents whose activity status a year from the time of interview was in education or training but that nonetheless said they did not attend any training/education course during the previous year. Finally, there was the case of a respondent who during the previous year attended some kind of education or training course, but for which there was no information on the type of course attended. Given their inconsistency, these cases were excluded from the empirical analysis.

[3] The thresholds of reliability used by Lehmann and Wirtz (2004, p 7) are as follows:
• When the sample size is more than 50, the data are considered reliable.
• when the sample size is between 20-49, the data are considered to show low reliability;
• when the sample size is less than 20, then information is not considered reliable.

[4] Bearing in mind that during this period there was a noticeable increase in investment in ALMP in both countries (see Chapter Five), one cannot exclude the possibility that, within this timeframe, the percentage of individuals in work might be influenced by the level of the investment in ALMP.

[5] However, as before, one cannot exclude the possibility that this might be related to an increase in opportunities to participate in education/training courses or job creation schemes in those countries.

The employment effectiveness of minimum income schemes and their respect for the right to personal development

Having measured the schemes' employment effectiveness and their respect for recipients' right to personal development, this chapter now uses simple correlational tools, QCA and cluster analysis to test the hypothesis that minimum income schemes that show more respect for the right to personal development, once labour market conditions are accounted for, will present higher levels of employment effectiveness.

Correlational analysis

As can be seen from Table 7.1, there is no systematic relationship between a scheme's respect for the right to personal development and their marginal employment effectiveness. Therefore we cannot corroborate the hypothesis posed earlier. This reflects the variety of situations found in the sample under analysis. For instance, the ABW in the Netherlands, which shows the highest respect for the right to personal development, presents negative marginal employment effectiveness. At the same time, the RMI in France and RMG in Portugal, which show the least respect for recipients' right to personal development, also display negative marginal effectiveness. On the other hand, the SB in Denmark, after the introduction of the new Act of Active Social Policy, is able to combine positive marginal employment effectiveness with a greater respect for recipients' right to personal development.

Table 7.1 also suggests that improving the satisfaction of the recipients' income needs and reducing the level of discretion they are subjected to can have a positive impact on the schemes' marginal employment effectiveness. On the other hand, increasing recipients' freedom to choose the job they want and, in particular, the type of activities they would like to perform, would have the opposite effect. Curiously, the data suggest that increasing the restitutive character of the sanctions applicable to minimum income recipients will not have an impact on the schemes' marginal employment effectiveness.

Finally, Table 7.1 shows that there is a positive correlation ($r = 0.17$) between the investment in training and education policies and the employment effectiveness of minimum income schemes. On the other hand, there is no correlation between the investment in job creation schemes and the schemes' ability to return beneficiaries

Table 7.1: Correlation between the employment effectiveness of minimum income schemes and their respect for the right to personal development

	Minimum income employment effectiveness[a]	Minimum income marginal effectiveness[a]	URC[a]
Satisfaction of income needs	−0.06	0.19	−
Freedom to choose other activities instead of paid work	−0.39	−0.31	−
Freedom to choose type of job	−0.11	−0.14	−
Freedom from discretion	0.12	0.17	−
Additional opportunities to work (A)	−0.06	−0.07	0.03
Opportunity to participate in education and training (B)	0.3	0.17	0.4
Opportunities to work and train (A+B)	0.13	0.05	0.24
Use of restitutive sanctions	−0.09	−0.06	−
Respect for the right to personal development	−0.08	0.02	−

Note: [a]Pearson correlation (*r*)

to the labour market. It should be noted, nonetheless, that there is a significant reduction in the impact of these variables on a scheme's employment effectiveness once labour market conditions are take into consideration. This seems to reflect the fact that there is positive correlation between the labour markets' URC and the total investment in ALMP (*r* = 0.24; see Table 7.1).

Bearing in mind the model developed by Layard and Nickel (1986),[1] which suggests that ALMP increase the ability of labour markets to create employment and reduce unemployment, this would suggest that there is a co-linearity between the investment in ALMP and the schemes' (non-adjusted) employment effectiveness. That is to say, investment in ALMP will increase the employment effectiveness of minimum income schemes both directly, by improving the employability of minimum income beneficiaries, and indirectly, in the sense that they improve the overall ability of labour markets to create jobs for unemployed people. As this makes it impossible to differentiate the direct effect of investment in ALMP in the employment effectiveness of minimum income schemes, it seems prudent to exclude the opportunity-related variables from the following stages of analysis.

Qualitative comparative analysis

Having tested the research hypothesis that guides this study using simple correlations, the next stage is to replicate this exercise, this time using Ragin's QCA. Bearing in mind the binary nature of QCA, the first step here is to identify the schemes that show more respect for recipients' right to personal development. In order to achieve this, it is first necessary to determine the criteria by which the various dimensions of this normative framework can be operationalised. Reflecting on the spirit of this normative framework and on the data available for analysis, it can be argued that:

- whenever a scheme secures recipients' an average disposable income that is equal or above 68% of the value of the poverty line,[2] income needs are better satisfied (see Chapter Five);
- whenever a scheme recognises the right to provide child or family care or to perform unpaid work in social economy organisations, it gives recipients more freedom to choose other activities instead of paid employment (see Chapter Five);
- whenever a scheme allows recipients to refuse a job on the basis of their previous occupation, or their level of qualification, it gives recipients more freedom to choose the job they want (see Chapter Five);
- whenever the funding and the administration of benefits is fully centralised, recipients have more freedom from discretion (see Chapter Five);
- whenever schemes do not impose the cessation of entitlement rights for the infringement of the activation requirements,[3] there is a greater focus on the restitutive character of sanctions (see Chapter Five).

Following the same line of reasoning, it can be argued that schemes that display positive marginal employment effectiveness are more effective at returning minimum income recipients to the labour market, whereas schemes that report negative marginal employment effectiveness are deemed as less effective.

Despite the preoccupation with reducing the loss of information involved in the creation of binary variables, there are some situations where this was unavoidable. For instance, the variable that identifies more effective minimum income schemes does not reflect the variations in the marginal employment effectiveness of the schemes, such as BSHG in Germany, ABW in the Netherlands, TTK in Finland, or JSA in the UK, where there were changes in the activation framework of minimum income recipients. Furthermore, this variable does not discern the strength of the schemes' marginal employment effectiveness. This is particularly problematic in those cases, such as RMG in Portugal and ABW before the introduction of the Jobseekers Employment Act, where the value of the marginal employment effectiveness indicator is close to 0. However, a sensitivity analysis shows that this loss of information does not affect the results presented here.[4]

The binary nature QCA also fails to capture some of the specificities of the French and Portuguese schemes. For instance, as Table 5.4 shows, minimum income recipients in France and Portugal are subject to a much lower level of discretion than those in Germany or Denmark (see Chapter Five). However, in QCA, RMI and RMP are included in the group of schemes where recipients are less free from discretion (see Table 7.2). Finally, QCA has some problems in capturing recipients' freedom to choose the type of activities they wish to perform in these schemes. For instance, the criterion adopted earlier does not acknowledge the possibility for recipients in some schemes, such as SB in Denmark, RMG in Portugal, or TTK in Finland, to provide care when there is no alternative form of provision.

Once the raw data have been recoded into binary variables, the various combinations can be put in a truth table. As can be seen in Table 7.2, the Irish SWA is the scheme that, under the binary lens of QCA, shows more respect for recipients' right to personal development. It should also be noted that the German and the Dutch social assistance schemes, even after the changes introduced in 1998 (see Chapter Four), show a comparatively higher respect for recipients' rights. In contrast, RMI in France and RMG in Portugal are the schemes that show the least respect.

The truth table also shows that, besides being the scheme that shows the most respect for recipients' right to personal development, the Irish SWA is one of the more effective at returning recipients back to the labour market. In contrast, RMG in Portugal and RMI in France not only show little respect for recipients' right to personal development, but also reveal problems in getting beneficiaries back to the labour market. This is not to say that there is a linear relation between the employment effectiveness of minimum income schemes and their respect for the right to personal development. For instance, ABW in the Netherlands and BSHG in Germany show more respect for recipients. However they are among the group that is the least effective at returning recipients back to the labour market. In contrast, TTK in Finland is one of the most effective schemes, but shows less respect for recipients' right to personal development.

Table 7.2 provides some additional information about the sample of cases under analysis that should not be neglected. For instance, it shows that there is more diversity in the cases that are more effective at putting recipients back into the labour market. This suggests that the employment effectiveness of minimum income schemes is a fairly complex phenomenon and depends on different combinations of causal conditions. Also, it shows that with the exception of Denmark, changes in the framework of the activation of minimum income recipients did not produce a qualitative change in the schemes' respect for the right to personal development. This explains why the 13 cases under analysis only produced eight combinations.

Table 7.2: Truth table on the causes that produce more effective schemes

Income needs are better satisfied	More freedom to choose other activities instead of paid employment[a]	More freedom to choose the job one wants[b]	More freedom from discretion	More focus on restitutive sanctions	More effective schemes	Cases
–	0	0	0	0	–	Dk – SB97
–	0	0	0	–	–	Dk – SB98
–	0	–	–	–	–	Irl – SWA98
0	0	0	0	0	–	Fin – TTK97, TTK99
0	0	–	–	0	–	UK – JSA97, JSA99
–	–	0	0	–	0	NL – ABW97, ABW99
0	0	0	0	0	0	Fr – RMI98; Pt – RMG98
0	–	–	0	–	0	De – BSHG97, BSHG99

Notes: [a] This set excludes all the cases, such as SB in Denmark, RMG in Portugal, or TTK in Finland, where recipients are allowed to provide care only when there is no alternative form of provision, and cases, such as JSA in the UK, where recipients with care responsibilities are only entitled to reduce the number of hours of work they are expected to perform.
[b] This set excludes ABW in the Netherlands, as it only provides a qualification-based exception for individuals with a university degree, which are not part of the traditional minimum income target population.

Finally, the truth table provides important information about the representativeness sample of cases under analysis. This is important in determining to what degree the results produced here can be extended to non-observed cases (Ragin, 1987, pp 104-6). Assuming that 32 combinations are possible[5] one can conclude that the eight combinations in the sample represent only 25% of all possible arrangements in the design of minimum income schemes. This suggests that we need to be extremely careful when trying to extrapolate the results of this analysis to non-observed cases.

Analysing the employment effectiveness of minimum income schemes

In line with the strategy defined earlier, the next step in this study is to identify the causal conditions (or combinations) that determine the effectiveness of minimum income schemes. As seen earlier (Chapter Four), this can be done by applying the Boolean minimisation procedures to the combinations that are more effective at returning recipients back to the labour market (MIEFF). This produced the following explanatory function:

MIEFF = INCNEED*freeemp*freejob*freedisc +
freeemp*freejob*freedisc*RESANCT +
incneed*freeemp*FREEJOB*FREEDISC*resanct +
INCNEED*freeemp*FREEJOB*FREEDISC*RESANCT

As can be seen, the minimisation procedure produced a fairly complex explanatory function. However, as Ragin suggests (1987, pp 110-11), this can be simplified with the help of Boolean factoring.[6] This produced the following explanatory function:

MIEFF = FREEDISC*freeemp*FREEJOB (incneed *resanct + INCNEED*RESANCT)
+
freedisc*freeemp*freejob (INCNEED + RESANCT)

This suggests that the ability of minimum income schemes to return recipients back to the labour market is conditioned by the structure which secures the delivery of the schemes. For instance, in more centralised (and therefore less discretionary) schemes, such as JSA in the UK and SWA in Ireland, as long as there are significant restrictions on recipients' freedom to choose the type of activity they wish to perform, they can offer better benefits, give recipients more freedom to choose the job they want and focus more on the use of restitutive sanctions and still be more effective.

On the other hand, more decentralised schemes, such as TTK in Finland and SB in Denmark, can only be more effective if they restrict the right of recipients to personal development. More specifically, decentralised schemes can only be more effective by restricting recipients' freedom to choose the type of activity and the job they wish to perform and by imposing either lower benefits or more repressive sanctions.

As well as highlighting the importance of the structure of implementation in explaining how respect for the right to personal development can condition the employment effectiveness of minimum income schemes, the explanatory function presented earlier suggests that restricting the freedom of individuals to choose other activities instead of employment is a necessary condition for more effective schemes. Most importantly, bearing in mind the types of restrictions imposed on the choices of individuals over the types of activities they wish to perform (see Chapter Five), this seems to suggest that minimum income schemes can only be more effective by restricting recipients' freedom to provide childcare.

We can further enquire into the factors that explain the success of more effective minimum income schemes by applying QCA's minimisation procedures to less effective policy combinations (mieff).[7] This produced the following explanatory function:

mieff = incneed*freeemp*freejob*freedisc*resanct +
INCNEED*FREEEMP*freejob*freedisc*RESANCT + incneed*FREEEMP*FREEJOB*
freedisc*RESANCT

As before, this can be further simplified:

mieff = FREEEMP*freedisc*RESANCT (INCNEED*freejob + incneed*FREEJOB) +
incneed*freeemp*freejob*freedisc*resanct

The first term of the explanatory function reinforces the idea that decentralised schemes that show more respect for right to personal development tend to be less effective at returning recipients to the labour market. Hence, whenever these schemes combine more freedom to choose the type of activities recipients can perform and a stronger focus on the restitutive character of sanctions with either higher benefits or more freedom to choose the job one wants, they become less effective at moving recipients back into the labour market.

The second term of the explanatory function, which can be seen as reflecting the experience of RMG in Portugal and RMI in France, seems to contradict some of the ideas about the factors that condition the effectiveness of more discretionary/decentralised schemes. Hence, despite offering lower benefits, imposing restrictions on recipients' freedom to choose the best way to exploit their talents, and imposing more repressive sanctions, these schemes fail to present higher levels of employment effectiveness.

However, rather than contradicting the results produced earlier, this second model seems to reflect the difficulties of QCA, given its rigid nature, to capture the specificities of French and Portuguese schemes. For instance, as mentioned earlier, the criteria adopted in the operationalisation of this normative framework does not acknowledged the possibility for RMG recipients in Portugal, to provide care when there is no alternative form of provision. In addition, one should also remember the possibility that we might be underestimating the freedom of choice exerted by RMI recipients in France (see Chapter Five).[8]

Another possible explanation is that QCA is failing to capture the impact of the structure of implementation in the schemes' effectiveness. As mentioned earlier, QCA does not capture the difference in the levels of discretion involved in the delivery between the French and Portuguese minimum income schemes and more decentralised schemes. As seen earlier (see Chapter Five), this can be explained by the specificity of the model of implementation adopted in these countries, which involves a high level of cooperation between national and local bodies. Given the complexity of these arrangements, one cannot disregard the possibility that the model adopted for the delivery of RMI and RMG is hampering the schemes' employment effectiveness.

Although there is no direct evidence of this, there is some evidence that this is hampering the delivery of insertion services to minimum income recipients. For instance, in Portugal, Cardoso and Ramos show that the central role of regional social security services in the Local Support Committees creates significant coordination problems in the delivery of services (Cardoso and Ramos, 2000, p 81). In France, Gautrat et al also report a lack of cooperation between the team of local integration counsellors and the PES (2000, p 112).

Validation of the research hypothesis

Having identified the factors that, under the lens of QCA, generate more effective minimum income schemes, we can now assess the empirical validity of the research hypothesis advanced earlier. As Ragin shows (1987, pp 118-21), the first step here is to determine if the research hypothesis is confirmed by empirical data. In order to achieve this it is necessary to map the areas of agreement between the research hypothesis (T'MIEFF), and the function that explains the success of the schemes that are more effective at putting recipients back in the labour market (MIEFF).[9]

Assuming that:

T'MIEFF = INCNEED*FREEEMP*FREEJOB*FREEDISC*RESANCT

and

MIEFF = INCNEED*freeemp*freejob*freedisc +
freeemp*freejob*freedisc*RESANCT +
incneed*freeemp*FREEJOB*FREEDISC*resanct +
INCNEED*freeemp*FREEJOB*FREEDISC*RESANCT

then

(T'MIEFF)(MIEFF) = (BASNEED*FREEACT*FREEJOB*DISCRET*RESTSANCT)
(INCNEED*freeemp*freejob*freedisc +
freeemp*freejob*freedisc*RESANCT +
incneed*freeemp*FREEJOB*FREEDISC*resanct +
INCNEED*freeemp*FREEJOB*FREEDISC*RESANCT)
(T'MIEFF)(MIEFF) = 0

As can be seen, this does not confirm the hypothesis that minimum income schemes that show more respect for the right to personal development, once labour market conditions are accounted for, are more effective at returning recipients back to the labour market. This obviously reflects the fact that restricting recipients' freedom to choose the type of activities they wish to perform is a necessary condition to produce more effective minimum income schemes. This is not to say that improving the schemes' respect for recipients' right to personal development will reduce their employment effectiveness. This is clear if we intercept the research hypothesis (T'MIEFF) with the explanatory function for less effective schemes (mieff). Assuming that:[10]

T'MIEFF = INCNEED*FREEEMP*FREEJOB*FREEDISC*RESANCT

and

mieff = incneed*freeemp*freejob*freedisc*resanct +
INCNEED*FREEEMP*freejob*freedisc*RESANCT +
incneed*FREEEMP*FREEJOB*freedisc*RESANCT

then

(T'MIEFF) (mieff) = (INCNEED*FREEEMP*FREEJOB*FREEDISC*RESANCT)
(incneed*freeemp*freejob*freedisc*resanct +
INCNEED*FREEEMP*freejob*freedisc*RESANCT +
incneed*FREEEMP*FREEJOB*freedisc*RESANCT)

(T'MIEFF) (mieff) = 0

This confirms the idea that, although the evidence does not validate the research hypothesis, neither can this be rebutted. In light of this, we can try to identify the shortcomings in the research hypothesis. The first step here is to identify the causal combinations that were not theorised by the research hypothesis (t'MIEFF). This can be done by applying Morgan's law to the combination that formalises the research hypothesis (T'MIEFF) (see Appendix C, this volume):

t'MIEFF = incneed + freeemp + freejob + freedisc + resanct

The next step is to intercept this with the function that explains the success of more effective schemes (MIEFF):[11]

(t'MIEFF) (MIEFF) = (incneed + freeemp + freejob + freedisc + resanct)
(INCNEED*freeemp*freejob*freedisc +
freeemp*freejob*freedisc*RESANCT +
incneed*freeemp*FREEJOB*FREEDISC*resanct +
INCNEED*freeemp*FREEJOB*FREEDISC*RESANCT)

(t'MIEFF) (MIEFF) = INCNEED*freeemp*freejob*freedisc*resanct +
incneed*freeemp*freejob*freedisc*RESANCT +
incneed*freeemp*FREEJOB*FREEDISC*resanct +
INCNEED*freeemp*FREEJOB*FREEDISC*RESANCT

This again highlights the idea that, contrary to what is hypothesised, minimum income schemes can only be more effective by restricting recipients' freedom to choose the type of activity they wish to perform. Nonetheless, as SWA in Ireland shows, if one excludes this variable, it is still possible for minimum income schemes to combine more respect for recipients' right to personal development with a higher employment effectiveness.

Cluster analysis

In line with the methodological framework defined earlier (Chapter Four), the final moment of this investigation consists of the use of cluster analysis to test the hypothesis that schemes that show more respect for the right to personal development, once labour market conditions are accounted for, are more effective at returning recipients to the labour market. Using the combined analytical power of hierarchical and K-means cluster analysis, the purpose here is to use the information on the internal consistency of the various clusters and the relative importance of the various variables in the clustering process to explain the differences in the employment effectiveness of the cases under analysis.

The first step consists in using hierarchical cluster analysis[12] to map the different arrangements in the respect for recipients' right to personal development in the cases under analysis. As can be seen from Table 7.3, this produced three different clusters. Bearing in mind that clusters here are aggregated according to the character of the sanctions regime and the level of discretion (see Table 7.4), the different schemes can be classified in the following way:

Table 7.3: Clusters of minimum income schemes

	Cases
Discretionary restitutive cluster	De – BSHG97
	De – BSHG99
	Dk – SB98
	NL – ABW97
	NL – ABW99
	Fin – TTK97
	Fin – TTK99
Discretionary repressive cluster	Fr – RMI98
	Pt – RMG98
	Dk – SB97
Non-discretionary restitutive cluster	Irl – SWA98
	UK – JSA97
	UK – JSA99

Table 7.4: Relative importance of variables in the clustering process (ANOVA analysis of variance)

	Cases
Satisfaction of income needs	0.443
Freedom to choose other activities instead of paid work	7.377
Freedom to choose type of job	7.575
Freedom from discretion	26.769
Use of restitutive sanctions	52.990

- *Discretionary restitutive schemes:* this cluster includes schemes, such as the Danish SB (after the introduction of the 1998 Act of Active Social Policy), BSHG in Germany, ABW in the Netherlands and TTK in Finland, which are delivered through a decentralised structure of implementation – and therefore give social workers more power of discretion over beneficiaries – and put more focus on the restitutory character of sanctions.
- *Discretionary repressive schemes:* this cluster includes schemes, such as RMG in Portugal, RMI in France and SB in Denmark (before the introduction of the 1998 Act of Active Social Policy), that are delivered through a decentralised structure of implementation and impose the termination of the right to a minimum income in the case of an infringement of the activation requirement.
- *Non-discretionary restitutive schemes:* this cluster includes schemes, such as SWA in Ireland and JSA in England, that are delivered through a centralised structure of implementation – therefore giving beneficiaries more freedom from discretion – and putting more focus on the restitutory character of sanctions.

If one focuses on the cases' distance from the cluster centre, which provides a good measure of the internal consistency of each cluster, one can conclude that there is a significant level of internal variation in the discretionary restitutive cluster (see Table 7.5) In contrast, there is a significant level of consistency in the non-discretionary restitutive cluster. Finally, Table 7.5 suggests that, despite integrating the same cluster, the Danish minimum income scheme (before the introduction of the 1998 Act of Active Social Policy) does hold some significant differences with regards to the French and Portuguese schemes.

Table 7.5: Cluster membership and distance from cluster centre

	Cases	Distance from cluster centre
Discretionary restitutive cluster	De – BSHG97	0.390
	De – BSHG99	0.390
	Dk – SB98	0.319
	NL – ABW97	0.300
	NL – ABW99	0.292
	Fin – TTK97	0.283
	Fin – TTK99	0.269
Discretionary repressive cluster	Fr – RMI98	0.230
	Pt – RMG98	0.245
	Dk – SB97	0.357
Non-discretionary restitutive cluster	Irl – SWA98	0.426
	UK – JSA97	0.267
	UK – JSA99	0.254

Analysing the employment effectiveness of minimum income clusters

Having identified the different arrangements in the respect for recipients' right to personal development in the cases under analysis, we can now look at how these might impact on the schemes' employment effectiveness. As mentioned earlier (see Chapter Four), this can be done by analysing the possible discrepancies in the marginal employment effectiveness of the cases in light of the qualitative aspects of cluster formation, namely, the internal consistency of the clusters and the relative importance of different variables in cluster formation. For instance, given the importance of the restitutive/repressive character of sanctions in the clustering process (see Table 7.4), we can conclude the character of the sanctions regime cannot explain the differences in the employment effectiveness of the cases included in the discretionary restitutive cluster.

This is also important in understanding the effectiveness problems in the French and Portuguese minimum income schemes. As can be seen from Table 7.6, although they use repressive sanctions to impose the obligation to exploit one's talents, these schemes are much less effective than the Danish SB, prior to the introduction of the 1998 Act of Active Social Policy. This has two implications. First, it refutes the idea that the employment effectiveness of these schemes is somehow related to the harshness of the sanctions imposed on recipients. Second, it reinforces the idea that the structure of implementation, which is the other key variable in the clustering process, might condition the employment effectiveness in the French and Portuguese minimum income schemes.

Table 7.6: Marginal effectiveness per cluster

	Cases	Minimum income marginal effectiveness
Discretionary restitutive cluster	De – BSHG97	–6.65
	De – BSHG99	–12.05
	Dk – SB98	4.15
	NL – ABW97	–1.29
	NL – ABW99	–5.75
	Fin – TTK97	6.45
	Fin – TTK99	8.97
Discretionary repressive cluster	Fr – RMI98	5.54
	Pt – RMG98	–9.58
	Dk – SB97	–1.36
Non-discretionary restitutive cluster	Irl – SWA98	3.55
	UK – JSA97	5.43
	UK – JSA99	

As seen earlier, there is a certain level of discrepancy between the Danish minimum income scheme, prior to the introduction of the 1998 Act of Active Social Policy, and the French and Portuguese cases (see Table 7.5). Looking back at the variables that measure the schemes' respect for recipients' right to personal development (see Table 5.8, Chapter Five), we can conclude that this discrepancy is mostly explained by differences in the level of discretion implied in these cases. In light of this, it can be again argued that the complexity of the structure of implementation of the French and Portuguese schemes might be hampering their employment effectiveness.

Reflecting on the evidence

Having examined the cases through the lens of simple correlations, QCA and cluster analysis, it is now possible to conclude on the empirical validity of the hypothesis that minimum income schemes that show more respect for the right to personal development, once labour market conditions are accounted for, are more effective at returning recipients back to the labour market. As the previous sections have shown, in a context where most minimum income schemes present low levels of employment effectiveness, the available empirical evidence has not confirmed this hypothesis. This is not to say that the hypothesis has therefore been refuted. As seen earlier, there is no systematic correlation between the two variables. In fact, with the exception of recipients' freedom to choose other activities instead of paid employment, schemes can combine higher levels of employment effectiveness with a respect for the right to personal development.

If we reflect on the various dimensions of this normative framework we can conclude that, as hypothesised (see Chapter Four), improving recipients' benefits will not reduce the employment effectiveness of minimum income schemes. In fact, in contrast with the argument that this could create unemployment traps (see Carone and Salomaki, 2001, pp 22-5), in the cases under analysis there is a positive correlation between the employment effectiveness of minimum income schemes and the disposable income of recipient households.

In contrast with what was hypothesised (see Chapter Four), restricting recipients' freedom to choose other activities besides paid employment is a necessary condition for increasing the employment effectiveness of minimum income schemes. In particular the evidence seems to suggest that minimum income schemes can only be more effective if they limit recipients' freedom to provide childcare. This suggests that the most powerful factor in explaining differences in employment effectiveness between the cases under analysis lies not on the strength of the sanctions, or on the investment in additional opportunities to work or to train, but simply on the priority schemes put on work as a means of social integration.

The impact of improving recipients' freedom to choose the type of job they wish to perform on the schemes' employment effectiveness varies according to the structure of implementation that secures the delivery of those schemes. For instance, in line with what was hypothesised earlier, centralised schemes can be more effective even if they give recipients more freedom to choose the type of job they wish to perform. On the other hand, when schemes adopt a more decentralised structure of implementation, increasing recipients' freedom seems to be associated with lower levels of employment effectiveness.

As hypothesised earlier, minimum income schemes can be more effective even if they reduce the level of discretion to which minimum income recipients are subjected. The most relevant point here, however, concerns the importance of the structure of implementation in explaining differences in the employment effectiveness of minimum income schemes. For instance, the evidence suggests that the complexity of the structure used in the delivery of the right to a minimum income might be hampering the employment effectiveness of the French and Portuguese schemes.

Most importantly, the evidence shows that, in comparison with centralised schemes, decentralised schemes can only be more effective by putting further restrictions on recipients' freedom to choose the job they wish to perform and by imposing lower benefits or more repressive sanctions. Unfortunately, there are no clear indications as to why this occurs, especially since none of these variables seems to have a particular role in explaining differences in the employment effectiveness of minimum income schemes. If anything, this suggests that more research on this topic is required.

Unfortunately, this study does not provide direct evidence to validate the hypothesis that increasing recipients' opportunities to work, or participate in education or training, will increase the schemes' employment effectiveness. However, there is some evidence that investment in ALMP can have a positive impact on the schemes' employment effectiveness. For instance, the evidence shows that the level of investment in education/training programmes, as it improves recipients' employability, can improve the employment effectiveness of minimum income schemes. Also, the evidence suggests that investment in ALMP, as they improve the overall ability of labour markets to create jobs for unemployed people, can have an indirect impact on the schemes' employment effectiveness.

Finally, the existing evidence also fails to confirm the idea that more repressive sanction regimes are more effective at putting recipients back in to the labour market. However, in contrast with what was hypothesised earlier, there is nothing to suggest that restitutive sanctions are necessarily more effective. This would suggest that more research on this topic is required, especially on the differentiated impact of the use of restitutive and repressive sanctions as a means to improve the employment effectiveness of minimum income schemes.

Conclusion

This chapter sought to test the hypothesis that minimum income schemes that show more respect for the right to personal development, once labour market conditions are accounted for, present higher levels of employment effectiveness. Considering the results produced by correlational tools, QCA and cluster analysis, the available evidence does does not confirm the research hypothesis advanced earlier. However, this does not mean that the hypothesis can therefore be refuted. In fact, the empirical analysis shows that, providing there are some restrictions on the recipients to choose other activities instead of paid employment, it is possible to successfully combine a greater respect for their right to personal development with higher levels of employment effectiveness.

Notes

[1] In a seminal study of the macro-economic effects of ALMP, Layard and Nickel (1986) develop a model that demonstrates that ALMP have a positive impact on employment. The effect of ALMP is twofold. On the one side, they enhance the size and employability of labour supply, which in turn facilitates recruitment and has a moderating effect on wages. On the other side, they reduce the friction between labour demand and labour supply, which facilitates the allocation of individuals to jobs (see, for example, de Koning, 2001, p 718). Although there is debate about this issue, there is evidence of the positive impact of ALMP in reducing unemployment (see OECD, 1993; Bellmann and Jackman 1996).

[2] This refers to the average value for all cases (see Chapter Five).

[3] This excludes sanctions related to the non-signature of an Insertion Contract/ Jobseeker's Agreement or the provision of false information concerning the recipient's financial situation (see Chapter Five).

[4] In order to eliminate the possible bias associated with this loss of information, a new analysis was performed, this time excluding the cases where there was a change in the terms of the right to a minimum income or to the framework for the activation of minimum income recipients (namely, De – BSHG99, Dk – SB98, NL – ABW99 and UK – JSA99), and where marginal effectiveness is close to 0 (Pt –RMG98 and NL – ABW97). However this has not produced any different results from those presented here.

[5] Following Ragin (1987, p 87), one can determine the total number of possible logical combinations by raising 2 to the power of ^{K}, where ^{K} represents the number of independent variables under analysis. In this particular case the total number of possible logical combinations of the variables that operationalise the right to personal development is equal to 2^5, that is 32.

[6] Boolean factoring involves the use of the commutative law, the associate law, the distributive law or the identity law. For further details, see Appendix C, this volume.

[7] In order to do this, it is first necessary to recode the output variable in such a way that less effective schemes are classified as 1, and more effective schemes are classified as 0. An alternative option here would be to apply Morgan's law to the explanatory function that identifies the casual conditions that produce more effective schemes (MIEFF) (see Ragin, 1987, pp 98-9). However, given the complexity of this explanatory function, this option was abandoned.

[8] The evidence on this issue is far from conclusive. A survey carried out by INSEE in 1998 showed that close to 90% of the insertion contracts signed in France

included job-search activities (see Lefevre and Zoyem, 1999, p 4). This would suggest that there is a great effort to induce recipients to take up jobs. However, this might just reflect the fact that social workers tend to prioritise more employable recipients in the signature of insertion contracts (Fraisse, 2002, p 18).

[9] For a more detailed description of the minimisation procedure, please contact the author.

[10] For a more detailed description of the minimisation procedure, please contact the author.

[11] For a more detailed description of the minimisation procedure, please contact the author.

[12] These clusters were produced using the 'complete distance' method, which is deemed to produce more robust clusters (see Maroco, 2003, p 304). In order to assess the impact of different clustering methods, the 'single linkage' method was also tested. However, with the exception with some minor differences with regards to the cluster centre distance coefficient, this produced the same outcome. In light of this, it was decided to keep the original cluster solution.

EIGHT

Conclusion

At the start of this book, it was argued that the introduction of activation requirements had raised two sorts of questions. The first refers to the way in which the provision of the right to a minimum income can be adequately justified. As seen earlier, this debate is centred on the question of whether the right to a minimum income should be made conditional on an individual's commitment to reciprocate this support by making a contribution to society (mainly through paid employment). This question entails two further issues. The first concerns the opportunities available to individuals for making a contribution to society. The second concerns the activities that can be considered to make a contribution to society.

Bearing in mind the variety of standpoints in the literature, we focused on the arguments posed by Mead and Van Parijs, which typify the fundamental standpoints in this debate, as a means to determine how can the right to a minimum income be adequately justified. We demonstrated that neither Van Parijs, whose argument for a basic income would unfairly favour those who do not want to work, and Mead, who fails to acknowledge the need for individuals to have an effective opportunity to contribute to society and the importance of some forms of non-paid employment (such care or voluntary work) as means to contribute to society, fail to provide an adequate justification of the right to a minimum income. Nonetheless, a closer look at the problems faced by both authors would indicate that a more satisfactory justification was possible.

Taking advantage of the ability of Durkheim's theory of social justice to conciliate social solidarity, personal development and social obligation, this book set out to develop an alternative normative framework to adequately justify the provision of a right to a minimum income. Based on a critical analysis of Durkheim's theory of social justice, it was argued that each individual has a right to exploit his/her talents, which can be exercised while performing a social function in society, such as paid employment, unpaid work in social economy organisations, providing care to dependent family members or improving his/her human capital through education or training. In order to secure this right, social actors and institutions must:

- meet the individual's basic consumption needs;
- eliminate direct and indirect constraints to the individual's choices on the best way to exploit his/her talents;
- provide the individual with opportunities to exploit his/her talents;
- enforce, through the use of restitutive sanctions, the individual's obligation to exploit his/her talents as to enable the personal development of others.

The provision of a right to a minimum income would therefore be essential in guaranteeing that individuals can exercise their right to personal development. However, in line with this framework, the exercise of this right to a minimum income is conditional on the performance of activities that could be seen to constitute an adequate form of exploiting one's talents, be it paid employment, participation in education or training, performing unpaid work in social economy organisations, providing childcare or care for dependent family members. Accepting that this obligation to exploit one's talents can be enforced through the use of restitutive sanctions, there is a requirement that individuals have effective opportunities to use their (recognisable) talents, to discover hidden ones (even including the transformation of impairments into new talents), or to engage in training or education.

The comparative advantage of this framework in justifying the provision of a minimum income can easily be demonstrated by confronting it with the proposals put forward by Mead and Van Parijs. For instance, in contrast with Van Parijs' unconditional basic income, this framework makes the entitlement to minimum income protection conditional on the obligation to exploit one's talents, thus avoiding favouring those who do not want to work (see Barry, 1992; White, 1997, 2000). On the other hand, in contrast with Mead, as it requires that individuals have effective opportunities to exploit their talents, this framework will not generate situations of unbalanced reciprocity (see Gutmann and Thompson, 1996; Etzioni, 1997). Furthermore, as it identifies a large range of forms of personal development, this scheme recognises the diversity of contributions individuals make to society, which Mead fails to acknowledge (see Gorz, 1992; Lewis, 1998).

Besides the issues regarding the most adequate justification for the provision of the right to a minimum income, the introduction of activation requirements also raised questions as to what degree the respect for recipients' rights could hamper the employment effectiveness of minimum income schemes. With this in mind, this book set out to determine whether schemes that show more respect for the right to personal development, once labour market conditions are accounted for, are more effective at returning recipients to the labour market.

Before going into a more in-depth analysis, one should again reference the factors that limit the generalisability of the empirical results produced in this study. For instance, despite adopting a methodological framework specifically designed to limit the negative implications this could produce, the analysis had to concentrate on a small number of cases (see Chapter Four). In addition, given the specificity of the methodological framework adopted in this study, the validity of results produced here is temporally bound (see Chapter Four). Therefore, we have to admit the possibility that any recent changes to the way that the right to a minimum income is defined, or in the activation framework of minimum income recipients, might generate new socio-institutional dynamics that can disrupt some of the causal mechanisms identified in this study.

In light of this, the results here should be interpreted with reference to the cases under analysis, and any possible extrapolations should be carefully contextualised.

Despite these limitations, this study does demonstrates that, with the exception of recipients' freedom to choose other activities besides paid employment, it is possible for schemes to combine more respect for their right to personal development with higher levels of employment effectiveness.

Lessons for policy

Reflecting on the results produced in this study, a number of issues can be identified that should be taken into consideration in future reforms of minimum income schemes in Europe. First of all, greater effort should be put into promoting the right of individuals to personal development. For instance, in countries such as Germany and Portugal, there should be an effort to increase the basic benefit rates so as to ensure that recipients have their basic consumption needs adequately satisfied (see Chapter Five). France and Portugal are countries where there is a significant need to reform the sanction regimes imposed on minimum income recipients, so as to emphasise their restitutive character (see Chapter Five).

There should be a greater effort to improve their freedom to choose the best way to exploit their talents. For instance, in France and in Portugal this means, as a first step, clarifying the rules that circumscribe recipients' freedom to decide what type of activities and what type job they can perform. In other countries, this means allowing recipients to provide childcare, care to dependent family members or to perform voluntary work in social economy organisations as an alternative to paid employment (see Chapter Five). In addition, more freedom should be given for recipients to choose the job that best matches their level of qualifications or previous experience. This is particularly the case of the French, Portuguese, Danish and Finnish schemes (see Chapter Five).

Second, there is a need to improve the employment effectiveness of minimum income schemes. As seen earlier (see Chapter Six), on average, only a quarter of the beneficiaries available for work are able to find a non-subsidised job within one year. This is a matter of concern as it means that a great number of recipients are still locked in unemployment or activation programmes that do little to improve their job prospects.

As well as highlighting the low employment effectiveness of minimum income schemes, this book provides a valuable insight into the factors that influence the schemes' ability to return beneficiaries back to the labour market. In particular, it highlights how the schemes' employment effectiveness is conditioned by the way policy makers circumscribe recipients' freedom to choose other activities instead of paid employment (see Chapter Seven). This exposes the clear policy choice that policy makers will be confronted with. They can follow the Danish example where increased employment effectiveness was achieved by limiting recipients' freedom to provide childcare, but complementing it with a strong investment in publicly provided childcare (see Mahon, 2002, pp 357); or they can choose to respects recipients' freedom to look after their children themselves, even if this has a negative impact on the schemes' employment effectiveness.

Notably, this book does not corroborate the literature on unemployment traps in income support benefits (see Carone et al, 2004). As mentioned earlier, this might be related to the fact that the job-search model that underpins the literature on unemployment traps assumes that individuals on minimum income are free to choose between taking a job and remaining unemployed (see Chapter Four). This appears to reinforce the claim made earlier that, rather than diminishing the benefit rates of minimum income schemes, more effort should be made to close the gap between recipients' disposable income and the poverty line.

This study has also shown that more repressive sanction regimes are not necessarily more effective in returning recipients back to the labour market. If anything, this seems to suggest that more restitutive sanction regimes are not only more respectful of recipients' right to personal development, but also give social workers more flexibility in the use of sanctions as a means to enforce recipients' obligations.

Any reforms to improve the employment effectiveness of minimum income schemes should take into consideration the schemes' structure of implementation. As seen earlier, the influence of particular policy variables, namely the way schemes circumscribe recipients' freedom to choose the job they wish to perform, varies significantly depending on the structure adopted in the implementation of minimum income schemes. No only that, as the evidence on the French RMI and Portuguese RMG seems to suggest, the structure of implementation can itself hinder the schemes' employment effectiveness.

Finally, and most importantly, this book has shown that the requirements of fairness and effectiveness are not necessarily contradictory. Where the cases under analysis are concerned, this study shows that, with the exception of recipients' freedom to choose other activities besides paid employment, many of the dimensions that measure respect for individual right to personal development do not hinder the employment effectiveness of minimum income schemes. However, rather than arguing for the possibility of restricting their freedom to choose, one should instead reflect on the centrality given to paid employment in the activation of minimum income recipients.

Going back to the debate on the right to a minimum income (see Chapter Two), this book has shown that the centrality given to paid employment as a form of reciprocating the support of society reflects a certain view of society where the market is assumed to be the main mechanism of social regulation. The right to personal development reflects a more comprehensive view of the functioning of society and a more critical view of the role of the market as a mechanism of social regulation. This provides the basis for a new understanding of activation. Rather than focusing on paid employment alone, this should cover a variety of activities that satisfy a social need, that is, that fulfil a social function. Besides opening ways for a broader spectrum for the personal development of individuals, this would have a positive impact on the functioning of society, thus reinforcing social solidarity.

Reflecting on recent developments

Although there are limits to the possibility of generalising the results produced in this book, nonetheless these provide an interesting basis on which to reflect on the latest developments in this domain. Without going into a comprehensive analysis of all the changes in the schemes under analysis, there are some developments that merit a more detailed analysis. The German case is especially relevant here as it involves a structural reform of the income support framework for unemployed people. The Hartz IV legislative package, approved in 2004, merged the social assistance and the unemployment assistance schemes in to one single scheme (Arbeitslosengeld II), targeted at unemployed persons who are not entitled to unemployment insurance and are able to work; and introduced a new minimum income scheme (Sozialgeld) that provides income support to all those in need and that are considered not fit to work (Zimmerman, 2006, p 37; Commission of the European Communities, 2007b).

Another relevant case is the reform of RMG in Portugal that, in 2003, was replaced by the *Rendimento Social de Inserção* (RSI), or social insertion income. Although it was claimed to put a stronger focus on the social insertion component of the scheme, the main changes consisted of the elimination of the automatic renewal of the benefit, which meant that recipients had to submit a new application at the end of 12 months on benefit, and a the tightening of eligibility rules for individuals aged aged between 18 and 30.[1]

Reflecting on the various developments in the recent decade, the suggestion is that, although this book has presented evidence that this will not necessarily increase the employment effectiveness of minimum income schemes, the reforms put in place have gone in the sense of restricting the schemes' respect for recipients' right to personal development. For instance, in the period between 2002 and 2004 in Denmark, a number of decisions were taken to reduce the benefits of social assistance recipients. This involved the imposition of a ceiling on social benefits to two-adult families with children and to single recipients aged under 25, and the reduction of benefits for people who received social assistance for more than half a year (Lind and Moller, 2006, pp 12-13).

Curiously, although this book has shown that this is the most influential factor in explaining differences in the employment effectiveness of minimum income schemes, there is no evidence of significant changes in the way schemes circumscribe recipients' freedom to choose other activities besides paid employment. This is not the case, however, regarding the rules that define recipients' freedom to choose the job they wish to perform. For instance, in Germany, in contrast with the previous legislation, recipients can no longer refuse a job on the grounds that it does not allow them to pursue their previous occupation. In fact, they are expected to take any legal job available (see Voges et al, 2001, p 78; Bruttel and Sol, 2006, pp 76-7).

Unfortunately, there is has also been no improvement with regard to the level of discretion to which recipients are subjected. In fact, the only noticeable event here refers to the increase in the level of discretion in the delivery of social assistance in the Netherlands. Whereas previously municipalities were expected to fund only 10% of the costs of delivery of ABW, from 2007 onwards they are expected to take full financial responsibility for the payment of social assistance benefits. Municipalities have also gained more freedom to define their own labour market programmes using block grants from central government (Bruttel and Sol, 2006, p 78).

Regarding the investment in the creation of opportunities for recipients to exploit their talents, the available data seem to suggest that, with the exception of Portugal, there was an evident decrease in the level of state investment in labour market policy (ALMP) in the countries under analysis (see Figure 8.1). However, if we take into consideration the variations in the percentages of unemployed individuals in the labour market and of the GDP per capita in the countries under analysis, we can conclude that this is not necessarily so (see Figures 8.2 and 8.3). For instance, bearing in mind that the level of unemployment has remained stable, the drop in expenditure in active ALMP as a percentage of GDP in Ireland seems to be more related with the increase in the overall performance of the economy than on a governmental decision to reduce the level of investment in this domain. On the other hand, the increase in the expenditure in ALMP in Portugal seems to reflect the significant increase in the number of unemployed people in the labour market

Nonetheless, the available evidence does suggest that there was a decrease in the creation of opportunities for individuals to exploit their talents in Germany. If we consider the comparatively slow growth in GDP per capita in this country, we would expect that the increase in the percentage of unemployed people would lead to a significant increase in the percentage of GDP allocated to the ALMP in this country (see Figures 8.2 and 8.3). However, as can be seen in Figure 8.1, this is in fact the country where the decrease in the level of public expenditure in ALMP is most evident.

Finally, although this book has not produced evidence that this can improve the employment effectiveness of minimum income schemes, a number of governments decided to increase the repressive character of the sanctions used in the activation of minimum income recipients. For instance, in Germany the sanction for a first infringement was increased from a 25% to 30% benefit cut (Voges et al, 2001, pp 86-7; Commission of the European Communities, 2007b). There was also a harshening of the sanctions for persistent misconduct. Whereas previously recipients could only have their share of the household benefit removed, the continuous failure of recipients to fulfil their obligations within a 12-month period could lead to the end of their entitlement (Voges et al, 2001, pp 86-7; Commission of the European Communities, 2007b).

A similar thing occurred in Denmark. Whereas previously every time a recipient failed to comply with their activation requirement they would be sanctioned with a fixed 20% benefit cut – under the 2005 Act of Active Social Policy continuous failure to participate in an activation measure or to report for a job opportunity

Figure 8.1: Public expenditure on ALMP as a percentage of GDP, between 2000 and 2005ᵃ

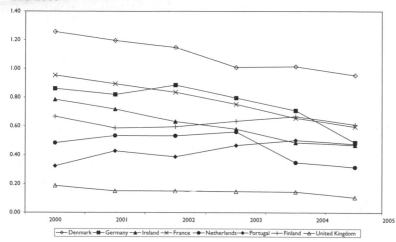

Note:ᵃ This includes expenditure on training, job rotation and job sharing, employment incentives, direct job creation and start-up incentives.

Figure 8.2: Unemployment rate between 2000 and 2005

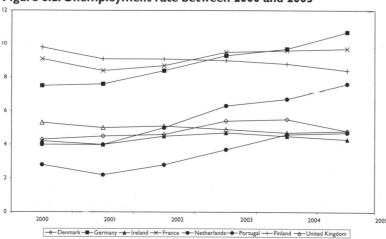

Figure 8.3: GDP per inhabitant, at market prices in euros, between 2000 and 2005

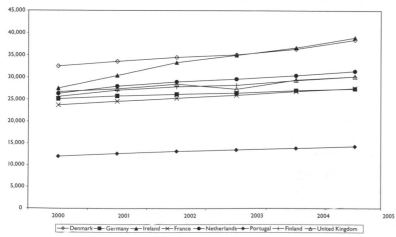

Source for Figures 8.1, 8.2, 8.3: Eurostat

121

could lead to the suspension of benefit. And, if a recipient participating in some kind of activation measure fails to show up, the benefit will be reduced in proportion to the hours and days of absence (Kildal, 2001, p 8; Commission of the European Communities, 2007b).

In the Netherlands, as part of a movement to give municipalities more power to define the terms of implementation of social assistance, the 20% maximum limit for a first infringement and the maximum one-month withdrawal of benefit sanction for continuous transgression of the activation requirement were dropped. Under the 2004 Work and Social Assistance Act local social services can now suspend benefit for recipients who fail to comply with the activation requirement (Commission of the European Communities, 2007b). In the UK, a new level of sanctions was introduced. As a consequence, in the case of a third failure to complete a New Deal Option a JSA recipient will be sanctioned with a 26-week benefit suspension (Saunders et al, 2001, p 2).

Opening new paths of research

As seen earlier, although it makes a significant contribution to understanding how respect for recipients' right to personal development can impact on the schemes' employment effectiveness, this book still leaves some unresolved issues that need further research. For instance, provided that adequate comparable data on this topic are available, it is important to analyse how recipients' socioeconomic characteristics and labour market history condition the relationship between the schemes' respect for the right to personal development and their employment effectiveness. Not only that, it is important to explore how this relationship is conditioned by the type of activation programme that is offered to recipients. Third, it is important to examine if, as Bloom and Michalopoulos's (2001) study shows, with a longer timeframe, schemes that place more emphasis on individual personal development can be as effective as those that are more labour market attachment-oriented.

Fourth, further research should go into how labour market conditions mediate the relation between the schemes' respect for the right to personal development and their employment effectiveness. In particular, it is necessary to examine to what degree this relationship is conditioned by the way in which labour markets are regulated. For instance, evidence shows that stricter employment protection reduces flows out of unemployment and increases the duration of unemployment (OECD, 1999, p 82; 2004, p 79). In this particular case, Table 8.1 does suggest the hypothesis that the employment effectiveness of minimum income schemes could be related to the level of employment protection in the labour markets they operate. This could, perhaps, explain the reason why Irish and British minimum income schemes can give recipients more freedom to choose the job they prefer and still rank in the group of more effective schemes. If anything, this highlights the need to analyse how the relationship between the employment effectiveness of minimum income schemes and their respect for the right to personal development is influenced by such features as the level of employment protection, the investment in ALMP, the level and structure of collective bargaining, the structure of the unemployment protection system, and so on.

Also, bearing in mind the suggestion made earlier that the activation of minimum income recipients should reflect a broader understanding of the functioning of society, and of the activities that recipients can be asked to perform, there should be further effort into researching how minimum income schemes enable individuals to pursue other forms of personal development besides paid employment. This entails a new understanding of the effectiveness of minimum income schemes that capture the abililities of individuals to participate in education or training, to provide care or to perform unpaid work in social economy organisations.

In addition, there are a number of topics that, given the purpose of this study, could not be covered here, but that deserve attention in the future. For instance, there should be further reflection on the type of scheme that can best support the right of individuals to personal development. In particular, it is necessary to investigate if this right can be best protected by a means–tested guaranteed minimum income, or by a universal benefit similar to Atkinson's 'participation

Table 8.1: Employment effectiveness of minimum income schemes and strictness of employment protection legislation

	Unemployment reintegration capacity	Marginal employment effectiveness	Employment protection late 1990s[a]
De – BSHG97	0.75	−6.65	2.6
De – BSHG99	0.70	−12.05	2.6
Dk – SB97	0.60	5.54	1.5
Dk – SB98	0.59	4.15	1.5
NL – ABW97	0.51	−1.29	2.2
NL – ABW99	0.47	−5.75	2.2
Fr – RMI98	0.74	−9.58	2.8
Pt – RMG98	0.59	−1.36	3.7
Irl – SWA98	0.66	3.55	1.1
Fin – TTK97	0.77	6.45	2.1
Fin – TTK99	0.71	8.97	2.1
UK – JSA97	0.65	5.43	0.9
UK – JSA99	0.65	2.58	0.9

Notes: [a] This indicator measures the weighted average of indicators measuring the level of regulation of regular employment, temporary employment and collective dismissals (for more information see OECD, 1999, Chapter 2).

Source: OECD (1999, p 66)

income' (1986). Furthermore, it is necessary to consider the role of asset-based redistributive policies, such as Le Grand's 'Accumulation of Capital and Education' (ACE) accounts (2006) or Stuart White's 'universal citizen's accounts' (2006) in promoting the right of individuals to personal development.

Finally, we need to consider what the possible implications are of the results of this book to the debate on the reform of social and employment policies in Europe, this debate has been fundamentally shaped by the notion of flexisecurity. Only just recently the Commission of the European Communities adopted a Communication entitled *Towards common principles of flexicurity: More and better jobs through flexibility and security* (Commission of the European Communities, 2007a).

The concept of flexicurity can be seen as an attempt to reconcile the need for further flexibilisation of labour markets and work organisations, seen as a condition to improve competitiveness and promote economic growth; and the need for socioeconomic security (see Wilthagen, 2002, pp 2-4; Tangian, 2004, p 17). The flexibility side of this binomium refers to employers' ability to adjust the number of employees to existing needs (internal numerical flexibility), to adjust the number and distribution of working hours (external numerical flexibility), to move employees from one task or department to another, or to change the content of their work (functional flexibility), and to adjust wages to existing competitive conditions (externalisation flexibility) (Tangian, 2004, p 16). Security, on the other hand, refers to the protection of employees against dismissal and significant changes of working conditions (job security), the ability of individuals to remain at work, even if not with the same employer (employment/employability security), income protection out of work (income security), and the ability to combine paid employment with other social responsibilities, namely the provision of care (combination security) (Tangian, 2004, p 17).

The relevant point here is that, in direct opposition to the evidence produced in this book, the concept of flexisecurity relies on the assumption that the promotion of economic effectiveness and the protection of citizens' social rights are fundamentally incompatible, and that the requirement for economic effectiveness should ultimately define the nature and extent of social rights. As this book shows, at the very least in what the activation of minimum income recipients concerns, this is not necessarily the case, nor does it need to be so.

This, of course, puts into question whether flexisecurity should be the golden standard that should guide the reform of social and employment policies in Europe. And it opens the way for the argument that increasing the respect for the right to individual personal development might be a good option to reconcile the need for economic effectiveness and social justice. If anything, this would suggest that further research should go on the impact of increasing the respect for individuals' right to personal development in other domains of social and employment policy such as the activation of unemployed people, hiring and firing legislation, work–life balance schemes, and so on.

Note

[1] Law no 13/2003.

Appendix A
Methodology for benefit comparison

Chapter Five uses the minimum income recipients' 'total household net disposable income' as a percentage of the poverty line as an indicator of the degree to which minimum income schemes provide a level of income that allows recipients to participate fully in society. The objective here is to clarify the methodology used to calculate this indicator.

Following relevant literature on the topic (see Eardley et al, 1996a, p 110), it was decided to compare the disposable income of four different households: a household headed by a single person; a household headed by a single parent; a couple without children; and a couple with children. Bearing in mind that these are not traditionally relevant in the population of social assistance beneficiaries, it was decided not to include a large household in this study (Kuivalainen, 2003, p 133).

In order to improve the reliability of the analysis, it was decided to introduce a number of restrictions in these family models. For instance, in order to exclude young adults who, in some countries, have lower benefit rates; and older beneficiaries, who might be entitled to non-contributory social pensions, the study compared adults aged 40. Also, in order to capture the impact of differentiated benefit rates of family allowances in the households' disposable income, it was decided to focus on children of pre-school age (3) and of school age (7). Considering the previous criteria, this comparative study focuses on four household types:

* single person, aged 40
* lone parent with two children (first child to be 7 and the second child 3 years old)
* couple (both aged 40) without children
* couple (both aged 40) with two children (first child to be 7 and the second child 3 years old)

The value of the poverty line was set at 60% of the median equivalised income (Eurostat, 2003b, p 3). In order to calculate the value of the poverty line for the different households, it was decided to use the 'modified' OECD (Organisation for Economic Co-operation and Development) equivalence scale, which gives a weight of 1.0 to the first adult, 0.5 to any other household member aged 14 and over, and 0.3 to each child (Eurostat, 2003b, p 1).

Table A.1: Poverty line for a single person

	Poverty line
BSHG97	1,410.20
BSHG99	1,437.75
SB97	6,726.13
SB98	7,063.78
ABW97	1,326.00
ABW99	1,418.62
RMI98	4,482.24
RMG98	56,364.88
SWA98	403.74
TTK97	3,734.60
TTK99	4,037.70
JSA97	446.03
JSA99	467.30

Source: ECHP

The calculation of the 'total household net disposable income' is based on a 'worst case scenario' assumption. Hence, recipients are assumed to have no income from work, unemployment benefits, earnings or capital. Therefore, the total household net disposable family income is the product of the value of the minimum income benefit and of any family allowance (where applicable), minus the share of taxes (where applicable).

As can be seen, there are two limitations to this definition of 'total household net disposable income'. First, it does not include the housing costs recipients might incur, or the housing benefits they might be entitled to. Accepting that this can cause some bias in the analysis, namely for countries such as the UK where housing benefit makes a significant part of the income of minimum income recipients, there are important reasons to justify this. First of all, there is a significant level of complexity in the measurement of housing costs, as they vary significantly with the structure of the household, the age and the location of dwellings (Kuivalainen, 2003, p 133). In the same way, there are significant variations in how different schemes cover housing costs (Eardley et al, 1996a, pp 67-71; Guibentif and Bouget, 1997, pp 29-31).

Second, despite some of the family models used in this comparison that include children in pre-school age, this notion of 'total household net disposable family income' does not include the costs families incur with childcare. This is due to the fact that, given the high percentage of private and informal provision, and the high level of local discretion, there is not enough comparative information available on this topic (see Bradshaw and Finch, 2002, p 80).

Table A.2: Disposable income as a percentage of the poverty line for a single person (aged 40)

	Social assistance benefit (A)	Housing benefits[a] (B)	Family allowances (C)	Amount before taxes (D=(A+B+C))	Taxation[b,c] (E)	Amount deducted[b] (F=(E*D))	TNDFI[d] (G=(D-F))	Poverty line (H)	TNDFI/ Poverty line (G/H)
BSHG97	538.00	0.00	0.00	538.00	0.00	0.00	538.00	1,410.20	0.38
BSHG99	546.00	0.00	0.00	546.00	0.00	0.00	546.00	1,437.75	0.38
SB97	6,825.00	0.00	0.00	6,825.00	25.00	1,706.25	5,118.75	6,726.13	0.76
SB98	7,104.00	0.00	0.00	7,104.00	25.00	1,776.00	5,328.00	7,063.78	0.75
ABW97	1,314.91	0.00	0.00	1,314.91	0.00	0.00	1,314.91	1,326.00	0.99
ABW99	1,399.50	0.00	0.00	1,399.50	0.00	0.00	1,399.50	1,418.62	0.99
RMI98	2,429.42	0.00	0.00	2,429.42	0.00	0.00	2,429.42	4,482.24	0.54
RMG98	22,100.00	0.00	0.00	22,100.00	0.00	0.00	22,100.00	56,364.88	0.39
SWA98	283.40	0.00	0.00	283.40	0.00	0.00	283.40	403.74	0.70
TTK97	2,021.00	0.00	0.00	2,021.00	0.00	0.00	2,021.00	3,734.60	0.54
TTK99	2,047.00	0.00	0.00	2,047.00	0.00	0.00	2,047.00	4,037.70	0.51
JSA97	229.37	0.00	0.00	229.37	0.00	0.00	229.37	446.03	0.51
JSA99	239.87	0.00	0.00	239.87	0.00	0.00	239.87	467.30	0.51

Notes: [a] Where available.
[b] Percentage.
[c] Where appropriate.
[d] Total net disposable family income.

Source: Commission of the European Communities (1998b, 1999, 2000)

Table A.3: Disposable income as a percentage of the poverty line for a lone parent (aged 40), with 2 children (aged 7 and 3)

	Social assistance benefit (A)	Housing benefits[a] (B)	Family allowances (C)	Amount before taxes (D=(A+B+C))	Taxation[b][c] (E)	Amount deducted[b] (F=(E*D))	TNDFI[d] (G=(D-F))	Poverty line (H)	TNDFI/ Poverty line (G/H)
BSHG97	1,183.60	0.00	220.00	1,403.60	0.00	0.00	1,403.60	2,256.32	0.62
BSHG99	1,201.20	0.00	250.00	1,451.20	0.00	0.00	1,451.20	2,300.40	0.63
SB97	9,100.00	0.00	1,400.00	10,500.00	0.20	2,100.00	8,400.00	10,761.81	0.78
SB98	9,472.00	0.00	1,525.00	10,997.00	0.00	0.00	10,997.00	11,302.05	0.97
ABW97	1,690.58	0.00	727.36	2,417.94	0.00	0.00	2,417.94	2,121.60	1.14
ABW99	1,799.33	0.00	727.36	2,526.69	0.00	0.00	2,526.69	2,269.79	1.11
RMI98	4,399.97	0.00	682.00	5,081.97	0.00	0.00	5,081.97	7,171.58	0.71
RMG98	42,200.00	0.00	8,400.00	50,600.00	0.00	0.00	50,600.00	90,183.81	0.56
SWA98	397.80	0.00	60.00	457.80	0.00	0.00	457.80	645.98	0.71
TTK97	4,689.00	0.00	0.00	4,689.00	0.00	0.00	4,689.00	5,975.36	0.78
TTK99	4,524.26	0.00	0.00	4,524.26	0.00	0.00	4,524.26	6,460.32	0.70
JSA97	460.83	0.00	0.00	460.83	0.00	0.00	460.83	713.64	0.65
JSA99	545.77	0.00	0.00	545.77	0.00	0.00	545.77	747.68	0.73

Notes: [a] Where available.
[b] Percentage.
[c] Where appropriate.
[d] Total net disposable family income.

Source: Commission of the European Communities (1998b, 1999, 2000)

Table A.4: Disposable income as a percentage of the poverty line for a couple (both aged 40), with no children

	Social assistance benefit (A)	Housing benefits[a] (B)	Family allowances (C)	Amount before taxes (D=(A+B+C))	Taxation[b][c] (E)	Amount deducted[b] (F=(E*D))	TNDFI[d] (G=(D-F))	Poverty line (H)	TNDFI/ Poverty line (G/H)
BSHG97	968.40	0.00	0.00	968.40	0.00	0.00	968.40	2,115.30	0.46
BSHG99	982.80	0.00	0.00	982.80	0.00	0.00	982.80	2,156.63	0.46
SB97	13,650.00	0.00	0.00	13,650.00	0.32	4,368.00	9,282.00	10,089.20	0.92
SB98	14,208.00	0.00	0.00	14,208.00	0.32	4,546.56	9,661.44	10,595.67	0.91
ABW97	1,878.50	0.00	0.00	1,878.50	0.00	0.00	1,878.50	1,989.00	0.94
ABW99	1,999.25	0.00	0.00	1,999.25	0.00	0.00	1,999.25	2,127.93	0.94
RMI98	3,671.14	0.00	0.00	3,671.14	0.00	0.00	3,671.14	6,723.36	0.55
RMG98	42,200.00	0.00	0.00	42,200.00	0.00	0.00	42,200.00	84,547.33	0.50
SWA98	456.73	0.00	0.00	456.73	0.00	0.00	456.73	605.61	0.75
TTK97	3,436.00	0.00	0.00	3,436.00	0.00	0.00	3,436.00	5,601.90	0.61
TTK99	3,480.00	0.00	0.00	3,480.00	0.00	0.00	3,480.00	6,056.55	0.57
JSA97	360.03	0.00	0.00	360.03	0.00	0.00	360.03	669.04	0.54
JSA99	376.37	0.00	0.00	376.37	0.00	0.00	376.37	700.95	0.54

Notes: [a] Where available.
[b] Percentage.
[c] Where appropriate.
[d] Total net disposable family income.

Source: Commission of the European Communities (1998b, 1999, 2000)

Table A.5: Disposable income as a percentage of the poverty line for a couple (both aged 40), with two children, aged 7 and 3

	Social assistance benefit (A)	Housing benefits[a] (B)	Family allowances (C)	Amount before taxes (D=(A+B+C))	Taxation[b c] (E)	Amount deducted[b] (F=(E*D))	TNDFI[d] (G=(D-F))	Poverty line (H)	TNDFI/ Poverty line (G/H)
BSHG97	1,587.10	0.00	220.00	1,807.10	0.00	0.00	1,807.10	2,961.42	0.61
BSHG99	1,610.70	0.00	250.00	1,860.70	0.00	0.00	1,860.70	3,019.28	0.62
SB97	18,200.00	0.00	1,400.00	19,600.00	0.33	6,468.00	13,132.00	14,124.87	0.93
SB98	18,944.00	0.00	1,525.00	20,469.00	0.33	6,754.77	13,714.23	14,833.94	0.92
ABW97	1,878.50	0.00	727.36	2,605.86	0.00	0.00	2,605.86	2,784.60	0.94
ABW99	1,999.25	0.00	727.36	2,726.61	0.00	0.00	2,726.61	2,979.10	0.92
RMI98	5,128.80	0.00	682.00	5,810.80	0.00	0.00	5,810.80	9,412.70	0.62
RMG98	66,300.00	0.00	8,400.00	74,700.00	0.00	0.00	74,700.00	118,366.26	0.63
SWA98	571.13	0.00	60.00	631.13	0.00	0.00	631.13	847.85	0.74
TTK97	6,104.00	0.00	0.00	6,104.00	0.00	0.00	6,104.00	7,842.66	0.78
TTK99	5,957.26	0.00	0.00	5,957.26	0.00	0.00	5,957.26	8,479.17	0.70
JSA97	568.17	0.00	0.00	568.17	0.00	0.00	568.17	936.65	0.61
JSA99	557.43	0.00	0.00	557.43	0.00	0.00	557.43	981.33	0.57

Notes: [a] Where available.
[b] Percentage.
[c] Where appropriate.
[d] Total net disposable family income.

Source: Commission of the European Communities (1998b, 1999, 2000)

Appendix B

Unemployment reintegration capacity (URC): sensitivity analysis

Table B.1: URC (sensitivity analysis)

	Inflow into employment	% of max (A)	Relevance of flow from unemployment to employment	% of max (B)	URC (A*0.8/ B*0.2)	URC (A*0.7/ B*0.3)	URC (A*0.6/ B*0.4)	URC (A*0.5/ B*0.5)
BSHG97	16.60	1.00	18.10	0.37	0.87	0.81	0.75	0.69
BSHG99	15.60	0.94	16.30	0.33	0.82	0.76	0.70	0.64
SB97	12.40	0.75	18.90	0.39	0.68	0.64	0.60	0.57
SB98	11.50	0.69	20.70	0.42	0.64	0.61	0.59	0.56
ABW97	8.30	0.50	25.70	0.53	0.51	0.51	0.51	0.51
ABW99	7.90	0.48	22.30	0.46	0.47	0.47	0.47	0.47
RMI98	9.50	0.57	48.80	1.00	0.66	0.70	0.74	0.79
RMG98	8.00	0.48	36.20	0.74	0.53	0.56	0.59	0.61
SWA98	11.60	0.70	29.70	0.61	0.68	0.67	0.66	0.65
TTK97	13.30	0.80	35.30	0.72	0.79	0.78	0.77	0.76
TTK99	12.20	0.73	32.30	0.66	0.72	0.71	0.71	0.70
JSA97	14.00	0.84	17.90	0.37	0.75	0.70	0.65	0.61
JSA99	15.10	0.91	12.80	0.26	0.78	0.72	0.65	0.59

Table B.2: Correlation between (non-adjusted) employment effectiveness and URC (sensitivity analysis)

	Y	URC (0.8/0.2)	URC (0.7/0.3)	URC (0.6/0.4)	URC (0.5/0.5)
BSHG97	21.43	0.87	0.81	0.75	0.69
BSHG99	14.71	0.82	0.76	0.70	0.64
SB97	29.85	0.68	0.64	0.60	0.57
SB98	28.00	0.64	0.61	0.59	0.56
ABW97	20.62	0.51	0.51	0.51	0.51
ABW99	15.07	0.47	0.47	0.47	0.47
RMI98	18.37	0.66	0.70	0.74	0.79
RMG98	22.50	0.53	0.56	0.59	0.61
SWA98	29.41	0.68	0.67	0.66	0.65
TTK97	35.09	0.79	0.78	0.77	0.76
TTK99	35.94	0.72	0.71	0.71	0.70
JSA97	31.03	0.75	0.70	0.65	0.61
JSA99	28.13	0.78	0.72	0.65	0.59
		$r = 0.31$	$r = 0.34$	$r = 0.34$	$r = 0.29$

Appendix C
Qualitative comparative analysis: laws of Boolean algebra

Laws of Boolean algebra

Commutative law

(a) $A + B = B + A$
(b) $A B = B A$

Associate law

(a) $(A + B) + C = A + (B + C)$
(b) $(A B) C = A (B C)$

Distributive law

(a) $A (B + C) = A B + A C$
(b) $A + (B C) = (A + B) (A + C)$

Identity law

(a) $A + A = A$
(b) $A A = A$

Redundance law

(a) $A + A B = A$
(b) $A (A + B) = A$

References

Ackum, A.S. (1995) 'Swedish labour market programs: efficiency and timing', *Swedish Economic Policy Review*, vol 2, no 1, pp 65-98.

Adler, M. and Asquith, S. (1981) 'Discretion and power', in M. Adler and S. Asquith, *Discretion and welfare*, London: Heinemann Educational.

Arriba, A. and Moreno, L. (2002) *Spain: Poverty, social exclusion and safety nets'*, CSIC Working Paper, no 02-10.

Atkinson, A. (1996) 'Citizen's income. The case for a participation income', *Political Quarterly*, vol 67, no 1, pp 67-70.

Avineri, S. (1968) *The social and political thought of Karl Marx*, Cambridge: Cambridge University Press.

Barry, B. (1992) 'Equality yes, basic income no', in P. Van Parijs (ed) *Arguing for basic income. Ethical foundations for a radical reform*, London: Verso, pp 128-40.

Bellmann, L. and Jackman, R. (1996) 'The impact of labour market policy on wages', in G. Schmid, C. O'Reilly and K. Schöman (eds) *International handbook of labour market policy and evaluation*, Cheltenham: Edward Elgar.

Bennett, A. (1999) 'Causal inference in case studies: from Mill's methods to causal mechanisms', Paper presented at the 1999 Annual Meeting of the American Political Science Association, Atlanta, Georgia.

Bloom, D. and Michalopoulos, C. (2001) *How welfare and work policies affect employment and income: A synthesis of research*, New York: Manpower Demonstration Research Corporation.

Bonnal, L., Fougère, D. and Serandon, A. (1994) 'L'impact des dispositifs d'emploi sur le devenir des jeunes chômeurs: une évaluation économétrique sur données longitudinales', *Economie et Prévisions*, vol 115, no 4, pp 1-28.

Bradshaw, J. and Finch, N. (2002) *A comparison of child benefit packages in 22 countries*, Department for Work and Pensions Research Report no 174, Leeds : Corporate Document Services.

Breen, R. (1991) *Education, employment and training in the youth labour market*, Dublin: Economic and Social Research Institute.

Breen, R. and Halpin, B. (1989) *Subsidizing jobs: An evaluation of the Employment Incentive Scheme*, Dublin: Economic and Social Research Institute.

Bruttel, O. and Sol, E. (2006) 'Work First as a European model? Evidence from Germany and the Netherlands', *Policy & Politics*, vol 34, no 1, pp 69-89.

Cantillon, B., van Mechelen, N., Marx, I and van den Bosch, K. (2004) 'L'evolution de la protection minimale dans les etats-Providence au cours des annees '90: 15 pays europeens', *Revue Belge de Sécurité Sociale*, vol 46, no 3, pp 513-49.

Capucha, L. (1998) *Rendimento Mínimo Garantido: Avaliação da fase experimental* [Guaranteed Minimum Income: Evaluation of the experimental phase], Lisboa: CIES/MTS.

Cardoso, A. and Ramos, G. (2000) *Integrated approaches to active welfare and employment policies: Coordination in activation policies for minimum income recipients – Portugal*, Dublin: European Foundation for the Improvement of Living and Working Conditions.

Carone, G. and Salomaki, A. (2001) *Reforms in tax-benefit systems in order to increase employment incentives in the EU*, Brussels: Commission of the European Communities, Directorate-General for Economic and Financial Affairs.

Carone, G., Immervoll, H., Paturot, D. and Salomäki, A (2004) *Indicators of unemployment and low-wage traps (marginal effective tax rates on employment rates)*, OECD Social, Employment and Migration Working Papers, no 18, Paris: OECD.

Clark, D. and McGillivray, M. (2007) 'Measuring human well-being: key findings and policy lessons', UNU–WIDER Policy Brief, no 3, Helsinki: World Institute for Development Economics Research.

Collins, E. (2000) *Integrated approaches to active welfare and employment policies: Coordination in activation policies for minimum income recipients – Ireland*, Dublin: European Foundation for the Improvement of Living and Working Conditions.

Commission of the European Communities (1998a) *Commission report to the Council, the European Parliament, the Economic and Social Committee and the Committee of the Regions on the implementation of Recommendation 92/441/EEC of 24 June 1992 on common criteria concerning sufficient resources and social assistance in social protection systems*, COM(98) 774, Luxembourg: Office for Official Publications of the European Communities.

Commission of the European Communities (1998b) *Mutual information system on social protection in the EU members and the EEA – 1998* (retrieved from http://ec.europa.eu/employment_social/soc-prot/missoc98/english/f_main.htm).

Commission of the European Communities (1999) *Mutual information system on social protection in the EU members and the EEA – 1999* (retrieved from http://ec.europa.eu/employment_social/soc-prot/missoc99/english/f_main.htm).

Commission of the European Communities (2000) *Mutual information system on social protection in the EU members and the EEA – 1999* (retrieved from http://ec.europa.eu/employment_social/missoc/2000/index_chapitre11_en.htm).

Commission of the European Communities (2007a) *Towards common principles of flexicurity: More and better jobs through flexibility and security*, Luxembourg: Office for Official Publications of the European Communities.

Commission of the European Communities (2007b) *Mutual information system on social protection in the EU members and the EEA – 2007* (retrieved from http://ec.europa.eu/employment_social/social_protection/missoc_tables_en.htm).

Cornilleau, G., Demailly, D. and Papin, J.-P. (2000) 'Les evolutions recentes du RMI: un effet perceptible de la conjuncture economique', *Etudes et Resultats*, no 86, pp 1-8.

Council Of Economic Advisers (1999) *Technical report: The effects of welfare policy and the economic expansion on welfare caseloads: An update*, Washington: The White House (retrieved from http://clinton3.nara.gov/WH/EOP/CEA/html/welfare/Techfinal.pdf).

Cox, R. (1998) 'From safety net to trampoline: Labor market activation in the Netherlands and Denmark', *Governance*, vol 11, no 4, pp 397–414.

Da Costa, A. B. (2003) 'Minimum income and basic income in Portugal', in G. Standing (ed) *Minimum income schemes in Europe*, Geneva: International Labour Office.

Dahl, E. and Pedersen, L. (2002) 'Workfare in Europe: does it work? Summary of a systematic review of effect evaluations of workfare programmes in six European countries', in I. Lødemel (ed) *Workfare in six European nations. Findings from evaluations and recommendations for future development*, Oslo: FAFO.

Dahrendorf, R. (1996) 'Citizenship and the social class', in M. Bulmer and A.M. Rees (eds) *Citizenship today*, London: UCL Press, pp 25-48.

Davies, K.C. (1971) Discretionary justice: A preliminary inquiry, Urbana, IL: University of Illinois Press.

De Haan, F. and Verboon, F. (2000) *Integrated approaches to active welfare and employment policies: Coordination in activation policies for minimum income recipients – Netherlands*, Dublin: European Foundation for the Improvement of Living and Working Conditions.

De Koning, J. (1993) 'Measuring the placement effects of two wage-subsidy schemes for the long-term unemploy(ed)', *Empirical Economics*, no 18, pp 447-68.

De Koning, J. (2001) 'Aggregate impact analysis of active labour market policy. A literature review', *International Journal of Manpower*, vol 22, no 8, pp 707-35.

De Koning J., Gravesteijn-Ligthelm, J. and Olieman, R. (1994) *AAJ: Meer dan een aai*, Rotterdam: Central Bestuur voor de Arbeidsvoorziening.

De Koning. J., van Nes, P., Zandvliet C., Donker van Heel, P. and Gelderblom, A. (1995) *Arbeidsvoorziening in perspectief. Evaluatie Arbeidsvoorzieningswet 1991-1994, Deelonderzoek B: resultaten en kosten (The Employment Service in perspective. Evaluation of the Employment Act 1991-1994, Part B: results and costs)*, The Hague: Ministry of Social Affairs and Employment.

Deacon, A. (2002) *Perspectives on welfare. Ideas, ideologies and policy debates*, Buckingham and Philadelphia, PA: Open University Press.

Defourny, J., Favreau, L. and Laville, J.-L. (2001) 'Introduction to an international evaluation', in R. Spear, J. Defourny, L. Favreau and J.-L. Laville (eds) *Tackling social exclusion in Europe: The contribution of the social economy*, Aldershot: Ashgate, pp 3-30.

Disney, R., Bellman, L., Carruth, A., Franz, W., Jackman, R., Lehmann, H. and Philpott, J. (1992) *Helping the unemployed: Active labour market policies in Britain and Germany*, Bonn/London: Anglo-German Foundation for the Study of Industrial Society.

Ditch, J. and Roberts, E. (2000) *Integrated approaches to active welfare and employment policies: Coordination in activation policies for minimum income recipients – United Kingdom*, Dublin: European Foundation for the Improvement of Living and Working Conditions.

Ditch, J., Bradshaw, J., Clasen, J., Huby, M. and Moodie, M. (1997) *Comparative social assistance: Localisation and discretion*, Aldershot: Ashgate.

Doyal, L. and Gough, I. (1991) A theory of human need, London: Macmillan Press.

Duncan, G. (1983) 'Political theory and human nature', in I.S.S. Forbes (ed) Politics and human nature, London: Frances Pinter, pp 5-19.

Durkheim, E. (1984) The division of labour in society, London: Macmillan Press.

Dworkin, R. (2002) Sovereign virtue. The theory and practice of equality, London: Harvard University Press.

Eardley, T., Bradshaw, J., Ditch, J., Gough, I. and Whiteford, P. (1996a) Social assistance in OECD countries: Synthesis report, London: The Stationery Office.

Eardley, T., Bradshaw, J., Ditch, J., Gough, I. and Whiteford, P. (1996b) Social assistance in OECD countries: Country reports, London: The Stationery Office.

Ebbinghaus, B. (2005) 'When less is more. Selection problems in large-N and small-n cross-national comparisons', International Sociology, vol 20, no 2, pp 133-52.

Enjolras, B. (2002) 'Workfare evaluation studies in France. Systematic review, in I. Lødemel (ed) Workfare in six European nations. Findings from evaluations and recommendations for future development, Oslo: FAFO.

Enjolras, B., Laville, J.-L., Fraisse, L. and Trickey, H. (2001) 'Between subsidiarity and social assistance – the French republican route to activation', in I. Lødemel and H. Trickey (eds) 'An offer you can't refuse': Workfare in international perspective, Bristol: The Policy Press, pp 41-70.

EPUNET (2005) ECHP User Guide, Colchester: University of Essex (retrieved from http://epunet.essex.ac.uk/ECHP_USER_GUIDE_28-11-2005.pdf)

Esping-Andersen, G. (1990) The three worlds of welfare capitalism, Cambridge: Polity Press.

Etzioni, A. (1994) The spirit of community. The reinvention of American society, New York: Touchstone/Simon and Schuster.

Etzioni, A. (1997) The new golden rule. Community and morality in a democratic society, London: Profile Books.

European Council (1992) Council Recommendation 92/441/EEC of 24 June 1992 on common criteria concerning sufficient resources and social assistance in social protection systems, Luxembourg: Office for Official Publications of the European Communities.

Eurostat (2000) Labour market policy database methodology, Luxembourg: Office for Official Publications of the European Communities.

Eurostat (2003b) The 'Laeken' indicators: Detailed calculation methodology, Luxembourg: Office for Official Publications of the European Communities (retrieved from www.cso.ie/eusilc/documents/Laeken%20Indicators%20-%20calculation%20algorithm.pdf).

Evans, M. (2001) Welfare to work and the organisation of opportunity: Lessons from abroad, CASEReport no 15, London: London School of Economics and Political Science.

Ferrera, M. and Rhodes, M. (2000) Recasting European welfare states, London: Cass.

Ferrera, M., Hemericjck, A. and Rhodes, M. (2000) The future of the European welfare state: Managing diversity for a prosperous and cohesive Europe, Report for the Portuguese Presidency of the European Union, Luxembourg: Office for Official Publications of the European Communities.

Fielding, J. and Gilbert, N. (2000) Understanding social statistics, London: Sage.

Fitzpatrick, T. (2001) Welfare theory: An introduction, Basingstoke: Palgrave.

Forbes, I.S.S. (1983) 'Conclusion', in I.S.S. Forbes and Steve Smith (eds) Politics and human nature, London: Frances Pinter.

Fraisse, L. (2002) 'Chapter 2. Executive summary: France', in I. Lødemel (ed), Workfare in six European Nations. Findings from evaluations and recommendations for future development, Oslo: FAFO.

Fraker, T., Nixon, L. and Losby, J. (1997) Iowa's limited benefit plan, Washington, DC: Mathematic Policy Research, Inc, retrieved from http://aspe.os.dhhs.gov/hsp/isp/iowalbp/Cover.htm#TOP

Frey, B.S., and Stutzer, A. (2002) Happiness and economics: How the economy and institutions affect human well-being. Princeton, NJ: Princeton University Press.

Gardiner, K. (1997) Bridges from benefit to work – A review, York: Joseph Rowntree Foundation.

Gautrat, J., Fraisse, L. and Bucollo, E. (2000) Integrated approaches to active welfare and employment policies – France, Dublin: European Foundation for the Improvement of Living and Working Conditions.

Geldof, D. (1999) 'New activation policies: promises and risks', in M. Heikkilä (ed) Linking welfare and work, Dublin: European Foundation for the Improvement of Living and Working Conditions, pp 13-26.

Giddens, A. (1971) Capitalism and modern social theory. An analysis of the writings of Marx, Durkheim, and Weber, Cambridge: Cambridge University Press.

Giddens, A. (ed) (1986) Durkheim on politics and the state, Cambridge: Polity Press.

Giddens, A. (1999) 'Risk and responsibility', The Modern Law Review, vol 62, no 1, pp 1-10.

Goldthorpe, J.H. (1997) 'Current issues in comparative macrosociology: a debate on methodological issues', Comparative Social Research, no 16, pp 1-26.

Gorz, A. (1992) 'On the difference between society and community, and why basic income cannot itself confer full membership of either', in P.Van Parijs (ed) Arguing for basic income. Ethical foundations for a radical reform, London: Verso, pp 178-84.

Gough, I. (2000) Global capital, human needs and social policies, New York: Palgrave.

Gough, I. (2001) 'Social assistance regimes: a cluster analysis', Journal of European Social Policy, vol 11, no 2, pp 165-70.

Gray, J. (1996) 'Mill's conception of happiness and the theory of individuality', in J. Gray and G.W. Smith (eds) J.S. Mill's on liberty in focus, New York: Routledge, pp 190-211.Gray, J. (1998) 'Introduction', in J. Gray (ed) John Stuart Mill. On liberty and other essays, Oxford: Oxford University Press, pp vii-xxx.

Guibentif, P. and Bouget, D. (1997) As Políticas Rendimento Mínimo na União Europeia (Minimum Income Policies in the European Union), Lisboa: União das Mutualidades Portuguesas.

Gutmann, A. and Thompson, D. (1996) Democracy and disagreement, Cambridge: Belknap Press.

Handler, J. F. (2004) Social citizenship and workfare in the United States and Western Europe: The paradox of inclusion, Cambridge: Cambridge University Press.

Hanesh, W. and Baltzer, N. (2000) Integrated approaches to active welfare and employment policies: Coordination in activation policies for minimum income recipients – Germany, Dublin: European Foundation for the Improvement of Living and Working Conditions.

Hanesh, W. and Baltzer, N. (2001) The role of social assistance as means of social inclusion and activation: A comparative study on minimum income in seven European countries, Report 4: Activation policies in the context of social assistance, Helsinki: STAKES.

Heikkila, M. (2001) The role of social assistance as means of social inclusion and activation. A comparative study on minimum income in seven European countries. Report 1 – Contexts, Helsinki: STAKES.

Heikkila, M. and Keskitalo, E. (1999) The implementation of workfare in social assistance and unemployment benefit schemes in Finland. The Finnish contribution to SEDEC WP3, Helsinki: STAKES.

Heikkila, M. and Keskitalo, E. (2000) Integrated approaches to active welfare and employment policies: Coordination in activation policies for minimum income recipients – Finland, Dublin: European Foundation for the Improvement of Living and Working Conditions.

Hollander, S. (1985) The economics of John Stuart Mill. Vol II. Political economy, Oxford: Basil Blackwell.

Holmlund, B. (1998) 'Unemployment insurance in theory and practice', Scandinavian Journal of Economics, vol 100, no 1, pp 113-41.

Hotz, V., Mullin, C. and Scholz, J. (2005) 'The earned income tax credit and the labour market participation of families on welfare', Joint Centre for Poverty Research Policy Briefs, vol 3, no 7.

Hudson, J. (1988) Unemployment after Keynes. Towards a new general theory, Hemel Hempstead: Harvester Wheatsheaf.

Hvinden, B. (1994) Divided against itself: A study of integration in welfare bureaucracy, Oslo: Scandinavian University Press.

Hvinden, B. (1999) 'Activation: a Nordic perspective', in M. Heikkilä (ed) Linking welfare and work, Dublin: European Foundation for the Improvement of Living and Working Conditions, pp 27-42.

ILO (International Labour Office) (2002) Learning and training for work in the knowledge society, Report IV (1), Geneva: ILO (retrieved from www.ilo.org/public/english/employment/ skills/download/report4.pdf).

ILO (International Labour Office) (2003) Key Indicators of the Labour Market (KILM). Third ed. [CD-ROM], Geneva: ILO

Janoski, T. and Hicks, A.M. (1994) 'Methodological innovations in comparative political economy: an introduction', in T. Janoski and A.M. Hicks (eds) The comparative political economy of the welfare state, Cambridge: Cambridge University Press.

Jones, R. (1986) Émile Durkheim: An introduction to four major works, Beverly Hills, CA: Sage Publications.

Jordan, B. (1996) A theory of poverty and social exclusion, Oxford: Polity Press.

Kangas, O. (1994) 'The politics of social security: on regressions, qualitative comparisons, and cluster analysis', in T. Janoski and A.M. Hicks (eds) The comparative political economy of the welfare state, Cambridge: Cambridge University Press.

Kildal, N. (2000) 'Workfare tendencies in Scandinavian welfare policies', Paper presented at the 8th BIEN Congress 'Economic Citizenship Rights for the 21st Century', Berlin, 6-7 October.

Kildal, N. (2001) 'Welfare policy and the principle of reciprocity', Paper presented at the ISA Annual Conference – 'Old and New Social Inequalities: What Challenges for Welfare States', Oviedo, 6-9 September.

Kruppe, T. (2001) 'Assessing labour market dynamics: European Evidence', ILO Employment Paper, no 15.

Kuivalainen, S. (2003) 'How to compare the incomparable? An international comparison of the impact of housing costs on levels of social assistance', European Journal of Social Security, vol 5, no 2, pp 128-49.

Layard, R. and Nickell, S. (1986) 'Unemployment in Britain', Economica, vol 53, pp 21-69.

Lechner, F., Reiter, W. and Riesenfelder, A. (1996) 'Anforderungsgerecht: Ergebnisse der Evaluierung des Beschäftigungsprogrammes "Aktion 8000"', Ergebnisse der innovativen Arbeitsmarktpolitik, Vienna: Wissenschaftsverlag.

Lefevre, C. and Zoyem, J.-P. (1999) 'Les contrats d'insertion du RMI: quelle perception en ont les allocataires?', DREES – Etudes et Resultats, no 45.

Le Grand, J. (2006) 'Implementing stakeholder grants: the British case', in E.O. Wright (ed) Redesigning distribution. Basic income and stakeholder grants as cornerstones for an egalitarian capitalism, London: Verso, pp 120-30.

Lehmann, P. and Wirtz, C. (2004) 'Household formation in the EU – lone parents', Statistics in Focus, no 5.

Levitas, R. (1996) 'The concept of social exclusion and the New Durkheimian hegemony', Critical Social Policy, vol 46, no 16, pp 5-20.

Lewis, J. (1998) 'Work, welfare and lone mothers', The Political Quarterly, vol 69, no 1, pp 4-13.

Lieberson, S. (1991) 'Small N's and big conclusions: an examination of the reasoning in comparative studies based on a small number of cases', Social Forces, vol 70, no 2, pp 307-20.

Lind, J and Møller, I. H. (2006) 'Activation for what purpose? Lessons from Denmark', International Journal of Sociology and Social Policy, vol 26, no 1/2, pp 5-19.

Lindley, R. (1986) Autonomy – Issues in political theory, London: Macmillan.

Lorentzen, T. and Dahl, E. (2005) 'Active labour market programmes in Norway: are they helpful for social assistance recipients?, Journal of European Social Policy, vol 15, no 1.

Lødemel, I. and Schulte, B. (1992) Social assistance: A part of social security or the Poor Law in new disguise?, Brussels: European Institute of Social Security.

Lødemel, I. and Trickey, H. (2001) 'A new contract for social assistance', in I. Lødemel and H. Trickey (eds) 'An offer you can't refuse': Workfare in international perspective, Bristol: The Policy Press, pp 1-40.

Lukes, S. (1973) Émile Durkheim – A historical and critical study, London: Penguin Books.

Lukes, S. (1977) Essays in social theory, London: Macmillan.

McKay, S. (2003) 'Working Families' Tax Credit in 2001', Department for Work and Pensions Research Report, no 181, London: Department for Work and Pensions.

Mahon, R. (2002) 'Child Care: Towards what kind of "Social Europe"?', Social Politics: International Studies in Gender, State & Society, vol 9, pp 343-79.

Maroco, J. (2003) Analise estatistica com utilização do SPSS (Statistical analysis using SPSS), Lisboa: Edicoes Silabo.

Marshall, T.H. and Bottomore, T. (1992) Citizenship and social class, London: Pluto Press.

Martin, J. (1998) 'What works among active labour market policies: Evidence from OECD countries' experiences, OECD Labour Market and Social Policy Occasional Papers, no 35, Paris: OECD.

Matsaganis, M., Ferrera, M., Capucha, L. and Moreno, L. (2003) 'Mending nets in the South: anti-poverty policies in Greece, Italy, Portugal and Spain', Social Policy and Administration, vol 37, no 6, pp 639-55.

Mead, L. (1986) Beyond entitlement. The social obligations of citizenship, New York: Free Press.

Mead, L. (1997) 'From welfare to work. Lessons from America', in A. Deacon (ed) From welfare to work. Lessons from America, London: IEA Health and Welfare Unit.

Meager, N. and Evans, C. (1997) The evaluation of active labour market measures for the long-term unemployed, ILO Employment and Training Papers, no 16, Geneva: ILO.

Milano, S. (1989) Le Revenu Minimum Guaranti dans la CEE, Paris: PUF.

Muhlberger, P. (2000) 'Defining and measuring deliberative participation and potential: a theoretical analysis and operationalisation', Paper presented at the 23rd Annual Scientific Meeting of the International Society of Political Psychology, Seattle, July 1-4.

Nelson, K. (2004) 'The last resort. Determinants of generosity of means-tested minimum income protection in welfare democracies', COMPASSS Working Paper no 21, retrieved from www.compasss.org/Nelson2004.pdf

Nicaise, I., Groenez, S., Adelman, L., Roberts, S. and Middleton, S. (2003) Gaps, traps and springboards in European minimum income systems. A comparative study of 13 EU countries, Leuven: HIVA.

OECD (Organisation for Economic Co-operation and Development) (1993) OECD Employment Outlook 1993. Growth and employment: A key role for human resource development, Paris: OECD.

OECD (1994) The OECD Jobs Study – Facts, analysis, strategies, Paris: OECD.

OECD (1998) The battle against exclusion, Vol 2. Social assistance in Belgium, the Czech Republic, the Netherlands and Norway, Paris: OECD.

OECD (1999) OECD Employment Outlook 1999: Giving youth a better start, Paris: OECD.

OECD (2003) OECD Employment Outlook 2003: Towards more and better jobs, Paris: OECD.

OECD (2004) OECD Employment Outlook 2004: Reassessing the OECD jobs strategy, Paris: OECD.

Oxford Research (2000) Integrated approaches to active welfare and employment policies: Coordination in activation policies for minimum income recipients – Denmark, Dublin: European Foundation for the Improvement of Living and Working Conditions.

Pavetti, L., Olson, K., Pindus, N., Pernas, M. and Isaacs, J. (1996) Designing welfare-to-work programs for families facing personal or family challenges: Lessons from the field, Washington, DC: Urban Institute.

Pedersen, L., Olsen, L., Wise, H. (2002) 'Report on findings from systematic review of Danish workfare/activation programmes', in I. Lødemel (ed) Workfare in six European nations. Findings from evaluations and recommendations for future development, Oslo: FAFO.

Plant, R. (2004) 'Can there be a right to a basic income', in G. Standing (ed) Promoting income security as a Right – Europe and North America, London: Anthem Press, pp 53-68.

Ragin, C. (1987) The comparative method: Moving beyond qualitative and quantitative strategies, London: University of California Press.

Ragin, C. (2000) Fuzzy-set social science, London: University of Chicago Press.

Rawls, J. (2001) Uma Teoria de Justiça (A Theory of Justice), Lisboa: Editorial Presenca.

Rihoux, B. (2006) 'Qualitative comparative analysis (QCA) and related systematic comparative methods. Recent advances and remaining challenges for social science research', International Sociology, vol 21, no 5, pp 679-706.

Roberts, B.A. (1990) 'The social construction of musical talent in music education students in Canadian Universities', Canadian Journal of Research in Music Education, no 32, pp 62-73.

Rosanvallon, P. (1995) La nouvelle question sociale: Repenser l'État-Providence, Paris: Les Éditions de Seuil.

Rosanvallon, P. and Fitoussi, J.-P. (1997) A nova era das desigualdades, Oeiras: Celta Editora.

Rosdahl, A. and Weise, H. (2001) 'When all must be active – workfare in Denmark', in I. Lødemel and H. Trickey (eds) 'An offer you can't refuse': Workfare in international perspective, Bristol: The Policy Press, pp 159-80.

Salonen, T. and Johansson, H. (1999) 'The Development Guarantee Programme – a case study of youth unemployment policies in Sweden', Social inclusion problems and policies: Case studies of policy and practice across 12 EU member countries, vol 2, SEDEC network.

Saunders, T., Stone, V. and Candy, S. (2001) 'The impact of the 26 week sanctioning regime', DWP/Employment Service Report no 100, London: Department for Work and Pensions.

Schomann, K. and Kruppe, T. (1996) 'The dynamic of employment in the European Union', Focus, no 55.

Schwartz, P. (1968) The new political economy of J.S. Mill, London: Weidenfeld and Nicolson.

Selbourne, D. (1997) The principle of duty. An essay on the foundations of the civic order, London: Abacus.

Sen, A. (1981) 'Rights and agency', Philosophy & Public Affairs, vol 11, no 1, pp 4-39.

Sen, A. (1993) 'Capability and well-being', in M. Nussbaum and A. Sen (eds) The quality of life, Oxford: Clarendon Press, pp 30-53.

Sen, A. (2001) Development as freedom, Oxford: Oxford University Press.

Smart, P. (1983) 'Mill and human nature', in I.S.S. Forbes (ed) Politics and human nature, London: Frances Pinter.

Smith, S.R. (2001) 'The social construction of talent: a defence of justice as reciprocity', The Journal of Political Philosophy, no 9, pp 19-37.

Spies, H. and van Berkel, R. (2001) 'Workfare in the Netherlands: young unemployed people and the Jobseeker's Employment Act', in I. Lødemel, and H. Trickey (eds) 'An offer you can't refuse': Workfare in international perspective, Bristol: The Policy Press, pp 105-32.

Spitznagel, E. (1989) 'Zielgruppenorientierung und Eingliederungserfolg bei allgemeinen Maßnahmen zur ABM', Mitteilungen aus der Arbeitsmarket und Berufsforschung, vol 22, no 4, pp 523-39.

Standing, G. (2000) Unemployment benefits and income security. Follow-up to the World Summit on Social Development, Geneva: ILO (retrieved from www. ilo.org/public/english/protection/ses/).

Standing, G. (2002) Beyond the new paternalism. Basic security as equality, London: Verso.

Swyngedouw, M. (2004) 'Review of "L'analyse quali-quantitative comparée (AQQC-QCA)" by Gisèle De Meur and Benoît Rihoux', European Sociological Review, vol 20, no 2, pp 161-2.

Tangian, A.S. (2004) 'Liberal and trade-unionist concepts of flexicurity: Modelling in application to 16 European countries', WSI Diskussionspapier, no 131, Düsseldorf: WSI.

Ten, C.L. (1996) 'Mill's defence of liberty', in J. Gray and G.W. Smith (eds) J.S. Mill's on liberty in focus, New York: Routledge, pp 212-38.

Theodore, N. and Peck, J. (2000) 'Searching for the best practice in welfare-to-work: the means, the method and the message', Policy & Politics, vol 29, no 1, pp 81-98.

Titmuss, R. (1971) 'Welfare "rights", law and discretion', The Political Quarterly, vol 42, no 2, pp 113-32.

Titmuss, R. (2001) 'The role of redistribution in social policy', in P. Alcock, H. Glennerster, A. Oakley and A, Sinfield (eds) Welfare and wellbeing: Richard Titmuss' contribution to social policy, Bristol: The Policy Press.

Torfing, J. (1999) 'Workfare with welfare: recent reforms of the Danish welfare state', Journal of European Social Policy, vol 9, no 1, pp 5-28.

Trickey, H. (2001) 'Comparing workfare programmes – features and implications', in I. Lødemel and H. Trickey (ed) 'An offer you can't refuse': Workfare in international perspective, Bristol: The Policy Press, pp 249-94.

Trickey, H. and Walker, R. (2001) 'Steps to compulsion in British labour market policies', in I. Lødemel, and H. Trickey (eds) 'An offer you can't refuse': Workfare in international perspective, Bristol: The Policy Press, pp 181-214.

Van Berkel, R. (2007) 'Social Assistance Dynamics in the Netherlands: Exploring the sustainability of independence from social assistance via labour market inclusion', Social Policy and Society, vol 6, no 2, pp 127-139.

Van Berkel, R. and Møller, I. H. (2002) 'The concept of activation', in R. Van Berkel and I. H. Møller Active Social Policies in the EU. Inclusion through participation, Bristol: The Policy Press, pp 45-72.

Van Oorschot, W. and Engelfriet, R. (1999) 'WORK, WORK, WORK. Labour market participation policies in The Netherlands – 1970-2000', Paper presented at 'The Modernisation of Social Protection and Employment' Conference, Florence (retrieved from www.engelfriet.net/richard/Work2.htm).

Van Parijs, P. (1997) Real freedom for all. What (if anything) can justify capitalism?, Oxford: Clarendon Press.

Voges, W., Jacobs, H. and Trickey, H. (2001) 'Uneven development – local authorities and workfare in Germany', in I. Lødemel, and H. Trickey (eds) 'An offer you can't refuse': Workfare in international perspective, Bristol: The Policy Press, pp 71-104.

Walker, R. (1999) 'Can work work? A preliminary assessment of the "welfare to work" strategy', Paper presented at the European Forum workshop 'The Modernisation of Social Protection and Employment – how to make social protection systems more employment friendly', Florence.

White, S. (1997) 'Liberal equality, exploitation, and the case for an unconditional basic income', Political Studies, vol XLV, pp 312-26.

White, S. (2000) 'Social rights and the social contract – political theory and the new welfare politics', British Journal of Political Science, vol 30, no 2, pp 507-32.

White, S. (2003) The civic minimum. On the rights and obligations of economic citizenship, Oxford: Oxford University Press.

White, S. (2006) 'The citizen's stake and paternalism', in E.O. Wright (ed) Redesigning distribution. Basic income and stakeholder grants as cornerstones for an egalitarian capitalism, London: Verso, pp 69-100.

Widerquist, K. (2001) 'Perspectives on the guaranteed income, Part I', Journal of Economic Issues, vol 35, no 3, pp 749-57.

Wilthagen, T. (2002) 'The flexibility–security nexus: New approaches to regulating employment and labour markets', OSA/Institute for Labour Studies Flexicurity Research Paper, no 2, Tilburg: Tilburg University.

Watts Miller, W. (1996) Durkheim, morals and modernity, London: UCL Press.

Zimmerman, B. (2006) 'Changes in work and social protection: France, Germany and Europe', International Social Security Review, vol 59, no 4, pp 29-45.

Wunsch, C. (2005) 'Labour market policy in Germany: institutions, instruments and reforms since unification', University of St. Gallen/Department of Economics Discussion Paper no 2005-06.

Index

Page references for tables and figures are in *italics*; those for notes are followed by n

Making it personal
Individualising activation services in the EU
*Edited by **Rik van Berkel** and **Ben Valkenburg***

"*Making it personal* provides a timely and authoritative engagement with debates about current transformations in social policy. The authors – and editors – are to be commended for producing this important, engaging and critical study." **Janet Newman, Professor of Social Policy, The Open University**

Public social services are increasingly being individualised in order to better meet the differentiated needs of competent and independent citizens and to promote the effectiveness of social interventions. This book addresses this development, focusing on a new type of social services that has become crucial in the 'modernisation' of welfare states: activation services.

The book discusses and analyses the individualisation of activation services against the background of social policy reforms on the one hand, and the introduction of new forms of public governance on the other. Critically discussing the rise of individualised social services in the light of various theoretical points of view, it analyses the way in which activation and the 'active subject' are presented in EU discourse. It compares the introduction of individualised activation services in five EU welfare states: the UK, Germany, Italy, Finland and the Czech Republic, focusing on official policies as well as policy practices.

The book provides original insights into the phenomenon of the individualised provision of activation services. It is useful reading for policy makers as well as for students and researchers of welfare states, social policies and public governance.

HB £65.00 US$99.00 **ISBN** 978 1 86134 797 8
234 x 156mm 296 pages February 2007

The Europeanisation of social protection

Edited by **Jon Kvist** *and* **Juho Saari**

The Europeanisation of social protection

Edited by
Jon Kvist and Juho Saari

"The relationship between the EU and national welfare states has become increasingly controversial. However, we lack systematic knowledge about the specific influences that the integration process is exerting on domestic social policies – and vice versa. This excellent book makes a step in this direction." **Professor Maurizio Ferrera, University of Milan**

Through eleven country studies, this book challenges the common view that social protection is exclusively a national concern with EU social policy fragmented and merely symbolic.

PB £25.00 US$39.95 **ISBN** 978 1 84742 019 0
HB £65.00 US$99.00 **ISBN** 978 1 84742 020 6
234 x 156mm 320 pages September 2007

Europe enlarged

A handbook of education, labour and welfare regimes in Central and Eastern Europe

Edited by **Irena Kogan, Michael Gebel** *and* **Clemens Noelke**

Europe enlarged

A handbook of education, labour and welfare regimes in Central and Eastern Europe

Edited by Irena Kogan, Michael Gebel and Clemens Noelke

"Europe Enlarged is essential reading for anyone interested in the social transformation of Europe at the turn of the millennium." **Robert Erikson, Professor of Sociology, Swedish Institute for Social Research**

This important new reference work describes the educational systems, labour markets and welfare production regimes in the ten new Central and Eastern Europe countries.

HB £75.00 US$135.00 **ISBN** 978 1 84742 064 0
240 x 172mm 384 pages tbc June 2008

The EU and social inclusion
Facing the challenges
Eric Marlier, Tony Atkinson, Bea Cantillon and *Brian Nolan*

THE EU AND
SOCIAL INCLUSION
Facing the challenges

Eric Marlier, A.B. Atkinson,
Bea Cantillon and Brian Nolan

"The EU Heads of State and Government have committed in Lisbon to making *a decisive impact on the eradication of poverty* by 2010. Even though the tools for fighting poverty and social exclusion rely primarily upon national actors, the Union is an active catalyst of their wills through sharpening diagnoses and highlighting the ways forward. The Union needs to become more aware of the linkages between its economic responsibilities and social cohesion. For this there is nothing more important than rigorous quantitative vigilance, of which this book is a clear illustration." **Jacques Delors, former President of the European Commission, 1985-1995**

This book provides an in-depth analysis of the EU Social Inclusion Process, the means by which it hopes to meet this objective, and explores the challenges ahead at local, regional, national and EU levels. It sets out concrete proposals for taking the Process forward.

HB £65.00 US$99.00 **ISBN** 978 1 86134 884 5
240 x 172mm 328 pages November 2006

To order copies of this publication or any other Policy Press titles please visit **www.policypress.org.uk** or contact:

In the UK and Europe:
Marston Book Services, PO Box 269, Abingdon, Oxon, OX14 4YN, UK
Tel: +44 (0)1235 465500
Fax: +44 (0)1235 465556
Email: direct.orders@marston.co.uk

In the USA and Canada:
ISBS, 920 NE 58th Street, Suite 300, Portland, OR 97213-3786, USA
Tel: +1 800 944 6190
(toll free)
Fax: +1 503 280 8832
Email: info@isbs.com

In Australia and New Zealand:
DA Information Services, 648 Whitehorse Road Mitcham, Victoria 3132, Australia
Tel: +61 (3) 9210 7777
Fax: +61 (3) 9210 7788
E-mail: service@dadirect.com.au